COMMUNICATION SEX & MONEY

MAJORING IN MEN®
The Curriculum for Men

Edwin Louis Cole

WHITAKER
HOUSE

T0043979

COMMUNICATION, SEX & MONEY WORKBOOK:
Overcoming the Three Common Challenges in Relationships

Christian Men's Network
P.O. Box 3
Grapevine, TX 76099
www.ChristianMensNetwork.com

Facebook.com/EdwinLouisCole

ISBN: 979-8-88769-151-0
Printed in the United States of America
© 2014 Edwin and Nancy Cole Legacy LLC

Published by:
Whitaker House
1030 Hunt Valley Circle
New Kensington, PA 15068

TABLE OF CONTENTS

Lesson 1
Man: The Glory of God

Lesson 1
Man: The Glory of God

I. **Introduction**

A. Fill in the two statements below with the following words: *(page 9)*

Christianity   legalizes   world   rationalizes   psychologizes   decriminalizes

What the _____ cannot control, it _____ and _____ .

What _____ cannot control, it _____

and _____ .

B. Why is conversion necessary? *(page 11)* _____

What is life's most precious commodity? *(page 11)* _____

C. What is a common complaint about men by both married and single women? *(page 12)*

_____

Principles I want to memorize:

Name the three common problem areas in relationships between men and women. *(page 12)*

1. _____ 2. _____ 3. _____

II.   **Man: The Glory of God (Chapter 1)**

A.   Fame can come in a _____, but greatness comes with _____. *(page 13)*
Name two things for which man was created. *(page 13)*

1. _____ 2. _____

B.   Marriage can be the closest thing to a _____ or _____ that we will ever have in this life. *(page 14)*

1.   Men and women were created basically the same to fulfill the same purposes on earth. *(page 14)*

___ True ___ False

2.   What are differences between men and women meant to do? *(pages 14-15)*

_____

3.   God created man for His glory and woman for the glory of man. *(page 15)*

___ True ___ False

For Further Study:

The difference is longevity – Revelation 2:26.

Man's glory – *"For thou hast made him a little lower than the angels, and hast crowned him with glory and honour"* Psalm 8:5; *"For I have created him for my glory"* Isaiah 43:7.

God created man with His characteristics – *"And God said, Let us make man in our image, after our likeness: and let them have dominion over the fish of the sea, and over the fowl of the air, and over the cattle, and over all the earth, and over every creeping thing that creepeth upon the earth"* Genesis 1:26; *"But the woman is the glory of the man"* 1 Corinthians 11:7.

C. For love to be love, what must there be? *(page 15)*_____

    1. If God had made Eve from anything other than what He had put in Adam, He would have made her an inferior being. Why? *(page 15)*

    _____

    2. What was Adam's "rib" symbolic of? *(page 15)*

    _____

    3. Marriage is the unifying of husband and wife into one flesh. *(page 15)*

    ___ True ___ False

    4. Read Genesis 1:26; 2:24; 5:2; 1 Corinthians 11:7 and 2 Corinthians 3:18.

D. Name a difference between the natures of men and women. *(page 16)*

MEN	WOMEN
_____	_____

Can a woman become the glory of her husband if her husband isn't becoming the glory of God by being

conformed to the image of Christ? *(page 16)* ___ Yes ___ No

For Further Study:

The rib God used to make the woman is symbolic of certain characteristics which God took from Adam to make the woman – the woman's nature – *"She shall be called Woman, because she was taken out of Man"* Genesis 2:23. The differences bring unity – Genesis 2:24; *"In the Lord, however, woman is not independent of man, nor is man independent of woman"* 1 Corinthians 11:11 NIV.

Bringing together the two in marriage – *"This explains why a man leaves his father and other and is joined to his wife in such a way that the two become one person"* Genesis 2:24 TLB; *"For as the woman is from the man, even so is the man also by the woman; but all things of God"* 1 Corinthians 11:12.

E.   Mediocre men want authority but not _____. *(page 16)*

F.   Excellence in spirit begins with having an excellent _____. *(page 16)*

    1.   The more Christ-like the man, the greater the _____. *(page 16)*

    2.   a.   Churchianity and Christianity are synonymous. *(page 16)*   ___ True ___ False

          b.   Reactions are not the same as results. *(page 16)*   ___ True ___ False

          c.   God wants results from men's lives. *(page 16)*   ___ True ___ False

G.   What is meant by this statement: "The method was instant and the touch was constant"? *(page 17)*

_____

_____

    1.   Describe the error of transposition. *(page 17)* _____

_____

For Further Study:

"I know thy works, that thou art neither cold nor hot: I would thou wert cold or hot. So then because thou art lukewarm, and neither cold nor hot, I will spue thee out of my mouth" Revelation 3:15-16.

Excellence in spirit – *"Then this Daniel was preferred above the presidents and princes, because an excellent spirit was in him; and the king thought to set him over the whole realm"* Daniel 6:3.

Christ-like – Ephesians 4:13

Mediocrity – *"Why do you call me, 'Lord, Lord,' and do not do what I say?"* Luke 6:46 NIV; Acts 19:13

The touch was constant – *"How God anointed Jesus of Nazareth with the Holy Ghost and with power: who went about doing good, and healing all that were oppressed of the devil; for God was with him"* Acts 10:38.

The touch is constant; the method instant – Acts 2:22. Teach touch, not method – Matthew 15:8-9.

Flesh cannot produce what the Spirit can – Isaiah 10:27; John 6:63.

2. You can get the same result from a "work of the flesh" as from the Spirit of God. *(page 17)*

___ True ___ False

Read: *"It is the spirit that quickeneth; the flesh profiteth nothing: the words that I speak unto you, they are spirit, and they are life"* John 6:36.

H. What is a "Microwave Christian"? *(page 17)* _____

_____

1. Men are made when the _____ of God _____ the dross out of their lives and

leaves them filled with _____. *(page 17)*

2. Read 2 Corinthians 4:17 and Hebrews 12:11.

Practical:

1. Read Psalm 8:5 and Isaiah 43:7. What do you think "man is created for God's glory" means?

_____

_____

For Further Study:

Mediocre Christians don't want to pay the price – 2 Corinthians 4:17; 1 Peter 1:7.

Temples of God – 1 Corinthians 3:16; 6:19; Colossians 1:27

Getting the dross out of our lives costs, but it is worth it – 2 Corinthians 4:17; Hebrews 12:11.

God reveals Himself to you – 1 Peter 2:9.

"Whereby are given unto us exceeding great and precious promises: that by these ye might be partakers of the divine nature, having escaped the corruption that is in the world through lust" 2 Peter 1:4.

2. **In your own words,** explain the difference between being alone and being lonely. _____

    _____

    _____

3. What are some immediate areas that you can begin to work on to have an "excellent spirit"?

    _____

Repeat this prayer out loud:

Father, You created me for Your glory. Help me to purify my heart. I choose to purge myself of those things that offend You and hamper my manhood, and by faith, I ask for the grace to have excellence of spirit. Lord, help me to realize the uniqueness of my own life and my wife's. Help me to recognize the worth and value of the woman with whom I have a marriage covenant. In Jesus' Name, Amen.

Principles I want to memorize:

Self Test *Lesson 1*

1. Fame can come in a moment, but _____.

2. Marriage can be the closest thing to a heaven or hell you will ever experience in this life.

    ___ True ___ False

3. God created man in His image for His glory and created the woman: *(circle one)*

    a. for the enjoyment of the man.

    b. for the glory of the man.

    c. to take care of the man.

4. Summarize God's purpose in creating man and woman with "differences."

    _____

5. The "rib" that God removed from man to make woman was symbolic of what?

    _____

6. Mediocre men want authority without: *(circle one)*

    a. marriage.

    b. position.

    c. accountability.

7. Becoming a Christ-like man is a quick and easy process.

    ___ True ___ False

Keep this test for your own records

Lesson 2
The Uniqueness of Woman &
Communicating with God

Lesson 2
The Uniqueness of Woman & Communicating with God

I.   **The Uniqueness of Woman (Chapter 2)**

    A.   The desires men and women have are basically satisfied in the same way. *(page 19)*

        ___ True ___ False

        Israel sinned by dealing with God as if He were a _____. *(page 19)*

        Men err when they deal with _____ as if they were _____. *(page 19)*

    B.   Use the following words to fill in below: *(pages 20-21)*

        the harvest   the reproductive process   salvations   the sale   their job

        1.   Where do men receive their greatest satisfaction? _____

        2.   A man's basic satisfaction is found in _____.

        3.   Farmers derive satisfaction from _____.

        4.   Salesmen derive satisfaction from _____.

        5.   Preachers derive satisfaction from _____.

For Further Study:

"So God created man in his own image, in the image of God created he him; male and female created he them" Genesis 1:27. Adam was created perfect, in God's image – Genesis 1:26, 31. Adam's job was to steward the earth – Genesis 1:28.

"Blessed is every one that feareth the Lord; that walketh in his ways. For thou shalt eat the labour of thine hands: happy shalt thou be, and it shall be well with thee. Thy wife shall be as a fruitful vine by the sides of thine house: thy children like olive plants about thy table" Psalm 128:1-3.

"Thou madest him to have dominion over the works of thy hands: thou hast put all things under his feet" Psalm 8:6. The human reproductive process satisfies – Genesis 1:28. *"As arrows are in the hand of a mighty man; so are children of the youth"* Psalm 127:4 (also vs. 3, 5).

C. Love is greater than _____. *(page 22)*

    1. Name three things woman was designed to be. *(page 22)*

       a. _____ b. _____ c. _____

    2. Read 1 Peter 3:7. **In your own words,** what does it mean?

       _____

       _____

    3. Give a reason for the birth of the women's liberation movement. *(page 22)*

       _____

D. What can men do to minister to a woman's unique nature? *(page 23)*

    _____

II. Communicating with God (Chapter 3)

A. Good communication in life begins with _____. *(page 27)*

For Further Study:

Sex alone doesn't satisfy man's God-given responsibilities and character. *"Husbands, love your wives, even as Christ also loved the church, and gave himself for it"* Ephesians 5:25 (also v. 26).

The woman's uniqueness – *"Likewise, ye husbands, dwell with them according to knowledge, giving honour unto the wife, as unto the weaker vessel, and as being heirs together of the grace of life; that your prayers be not hindered"* 1 Peter 3:7.

Don't worship the creature – *"They exchanged the truth of God for a lie, and worshiped and served created things rather than the Creator – who is forever praised. Amen"* Romans 1:25 NIV.

"Husbands, love your wives, and be not bitter against them" Colossians 3:19.

"You husbands must be careful of your wives, being thoughtful of their needs and honoring them as the weaker sex … giving honour unto the wife, as unto the weaker vessel, and as being heirs together of the grace of life" 1 Peter 3:7 TLB, KJV.

"Live joyfully with the wife whom thou lovest all the days of the life of thy vanity" Ecclesiastes 9:9.

B.   Read the "parable of the sower" in Mark 4:1-20.

    1.   When God gives His Word, what immediately happens? *(page 27)*

_____

    2.   Mark all of the following that are Biblical stories of people who experienced probationary periods: *(pages 27-28)*

         _____   Adam and Eve   _____   Paul   _____   Moses

         _____   Elijah   _____   Titus   _____   Jesus

        (See Genesis 3, Exodus 15, 1 Kings 19 and Luke 4, and find more if you can!)

    3.   Which is more important? *(check one)* *(page 28)*

        ____ the day before a battle   ____ the day after a battle

        In your opinion, why is this?

_____

_____

        Read 1 Corinthians 10:12.

For Further Study:

"Those along the path are the ones who hear, and then the devil comes and takes away the word from their hearts, so that they may not believe and be saved" Luke 8:12 NIV.

Examples of God's probationary period – Genesis 3:1-5; Exodus 15:5-7; 1 Kings 19:1-3

Immediately after His baptism, Jesus was tempted of the devil in the wilderness. *"And Jesus being full of the Holy Ghost returned from Jordan, and was led by the Spirit into the wilderness, Being forty days tempted of the devil ... And the devil said unto him, If thou be the Son of God, command this stone that it be made bread ... And when the devil had ended all the temptation, he departed from him for a season. And Jesus returned in the power of the Spirit into Galilee: and there went out a fame of him through all the region round about"* Luke 4:1-3, 13-14. Take heed lest we fall – 1 Corinthians 10:12.

4.   Do you believe everything God says?   ___ Yes ___ No

      Can others believe everything you say?   ___ Yes ___ No

5.   Name the greatest evidence of loving God. *(page 29)* _____

C.   Use the following to fill in the sentences below: *(page 29)*

truth   pride   lie   unbelief   deceitfulness   lying

1.   No _____ can serve the purposes of God.

2.   _____ is the basis of sin.

3.   _____ is the strength of sin.

4.   _____ is the character of sin.

5.   All deceitfulness is a form of _____.

For Further Study:

Satan wants to destroy our word – Mark 4:15; John 10:10.

We must watch our word – Colossians 4:6; Titus 1:16; James 3:2.

"Keep control of your tongue, and guard your lips from telling lies" 1 Peter 3:10 TLB.

A man may have a passion for God but not love God – Proverbs 26:23; Ezekiel 33:31; Romans 1:21; 2:23-24; Revelation 2:4, 5.

"He that hath my commandments, and keepeth them, he it is that loveth me" John 14:21.

"If ye keep my commandments, ye shall abide in my love" John 15:10.

Deception and lies – Psalm 120:2; Proverbs 12:22; 2 Corinthians 11:14-15

Our hearts must have outside objective truth – Psalms 19:12; 139:23, 24; Jeremiah 17:9; John 4:23-24; 16:13; Acts 24:16; Romans 9:1.

"If we walk in the light, as he is in the light, we have fellowship one with another" 1 John 1:7.

D. **In your own words,** define prayer. *(page 30)* _____

_____

1. Circle everything prayer is. *(page 30)*

    acknowledging the authority of Christ   submitting to the will of God

    talking God into blessing me   taking dominion over matters

    exercising faith in the Word of God   receiving His counsel

    subjugating the flesh   begging God to change my wife

    a means to getting my own way   subduing Satan

    causing the Kingdom of God to be
    established on the earth as it is in Heaven

For Further Study:

"If ye abide in me, and my words abide in you, ye shall ask what ye will, and it shall be done unto you" John 15:7.
Prayer is not an attempt to convince God of our righteousness, but an opportunity for God to show us His righteousness – Isaiah 6:5; Luke 14:10-14.
Authentic prayer is dealing with matters of Heaven and Hell based on the Word of God – Ezekiel 22:30; Luke 17:6.
The authority of Christ – Luke 9:1; 10:19; Submitting to God's will – Psalm 143:10; John 5:14; Taking dominion – Matthew 16:18-19; Exercising faith – John 14:12; Receiving God's counsel – James 1:5; Subjugating the flesh – James 4:2; Subduing Satan – 1 John 3:8; Establishing the Kingdom of God – Matthew 6:10
"The effectual fervent prayer of a righteous man availeth much" James 5:16; 2 Chronicles 7:14; *"Men ought always to pray, and not to faint"* Luke 18:1; Isaiah 64:7.

2.   Satan _____ at Christians' wishes, but trembles at their _____.
     (page 30)

Practical:

1.   Has Satan ever stolen God's Word from you? Has he stolen your word? When?

     _____

2.   Read: *"And I sought for a man among them, that should make up the hedge, and stand in the gap before me for the land, that I should not destroy it"* Ezekiel 22:30.

3.   Be honest with yourself, and keep a prayer diary for one week. Use the results to find ways to improve your prayer life.

Repeat this prayer out loud:

Father, in Jesus' Name, I am determined to make my word sacred to me, just as Yours is to You. Please forgive me for taking my own word so lightly and especially for allowing Satan to steal Your Word from me. Help me remember that I need to pray throughout the day, and please help me pray. I invite You to remind me at any time. Thank You for waiting for me to get to this point. Amen.

For Further Study:

At the cross, men find freedom – Colossians 2:13-15. Men find the Lord waiting for them – Matthew 6:6.
Be honest with God – *"Behold, thou desirest truth in the inward parts: and in the hidden part thou shalt make me to know wisdom"* Psalm 51:6.
"Oh Lord, thou hast searched me, and known me. Thou knowest my downsitting and mine uprising, thou understandest my thought afar off ... Whither shall I go from thy spirit? or whither shall I flee from thy presence?" Psalm 139:1-7.
"Neither is there any creature that is not manifest in his sight: but all things are naked and opened unto the eyes of him with whom we have to do" Hebrews 4:13.
God fills you with Himself – *"Draw nigh to God, and he will draw nigh to you"* James 4:8-10.
"Be filled with the Spirit" Ephesians 5:18.
"In everything by prayer and supplication with thanksgiving let your requests be made known to God" Philippians 4:6-7.
God will never let you down – Psalm 27:10; Matthew 11:28; Hebrews 13:5.

Self Test *Lesson 2*

1. One of Israel's sins was dealing with God as if He were a _____.

2. Adam's unique nature and desire were basically satisfied how?

   _____

3. The ability of men to procreate is a true sign of real manhood. ___ True ___ False

4. Christianity teaches that women should be subjugated and put down. ___ True ___ False

5. All good communication in life must begin with what?

   _____

6. Give some Bible examples of Satan attempting to steal God's Word.

   _____

   _____

7. What number in the Bible usually represents a "probationary" period? _____

8. Which is more important: the day before the battle or the day after the battle? _____

9. The closer a lie is to the truth, the more damning it is. ___ True ___ False

Keep this test for your own records

Lesson 3
Your Word Is Your Bond

Lesson 3
Your Word Is Your Bond

    A.   God never gives _____ without _____. *(page 34)*

        1.   Write out Deuteronomy 23:21.

        2.   Name one reason some Christians live unfulfilled lives. *(page 35)*

For Further Study:
Keeping your word to God – Deuteronomy 23:21; Proverbs 12:22; 20:25; Matthew 21:28-31
"A man may ruin his chances by his own foolishness and then blame it on the Lord!" Proverbs 19:3 TLB.
Keeping your word to spiritual leadership – John 13:20; Acts 5:3, 4
God holds us accountable for our words – Matthew 12:36.
A man's name is only as good as his word – *"A good man is known by his truthfulness; a false man by deceit and lies"* Proverbs 12:17 TLB; *"A good name is rather to be chosen than great riches, and loving favour rather than silver and gold"* Proverbs 22:1.

B.   Use the following to fill in the sentences below: *(page 35)*

faith   name   conduct   nature   word   character

1.   A man's _____ is only as good as his _____.

2.   A man's _____ is only as good as his _____.

3.   A man's _____ is the expression of his _____.

4.   God's Word is the sole source of our _____ and the absolute rule of our _____.

5.   Our word is a source of _____ to those who receive it, and it determines their _____.

Read aloud Proverbs 12:17 and Proverbs 22:1.

Do these describe you?   ___ Yes ___ No

C.   What part does truth play in becoming a man of your word?

_____

_____

For Further Study:

A man's word and character – Proverbs 21:8; 24:3, 4
"A good man out of the good treasure of his heart bringeth forth that which is good; and an evil man out of the evil treasure of his heart bringeth forth that which is evil: for of the abundance of the heart his mouth speaketh" Luke 6:45.
God's Word – Luke 21:33; John 1:1
Our word – Psalm 24:3, 4; Proverbs 25:13, 19
Truth is the essence of the Word – *"Every word of God proves true. He defends all who come to him for protection"* Proverbs 30:5 TLB.
The love of the truth is essential – *"They received not the love of the truth, that they might be saved"* 2 Thessalonians 2:10.
We have a crisis in truth today – *"And judgment is turned away backward, and justice standeth afar off: for truth is fallen in the street, and equity cannot enter"* Isaiah 59:14.

1. What it means to be holy is to _____ God, because the _____ of God is the criterion of holiness. *(page 36)*

2. Being a man of _____ is being a man of your _____. *(page 36)*

3. Define integrity *(use a dictionary or put in your own words).*

    _____

    _____

4. What happens when you punish your children for not keeping their word when you are guilty of the same? *(pages 36-37)*

    _____

5. *"The just man walketh in his integrity: his children are blessed after him"* Proverbs 20:7.

    Why are children blessed if their father is a man of integrity?

    _____

For Further Study:

Truth is popular in Heaven – *"The lip of truth shall be established for ever: but a lying tongue is but for a moment"* Proverbs 12:19; Proverbs 12:22; Isaiah 59:15; 2 Timothy 3:12-13.

Every man must be grounded in truth – *"Sanctify them through thy truth: thy word is truth"* John 17:17; *"Seeing ye have purified your souls in obeying the truth through the Spirit"* 1 Peter 1:22; *"And it is the Spirit that beareth witness, because the Spirit is truth"* 1 John 5:6; *"Howbeit when he, the Spirit of truth, is come, he will guide you into all truth"* John 16:13.

D.   Name three evidences of a changed life after conversion. *(page 38)*

   1. _____

   2. _____

   3. _____

E.   Knowing the truth and not living by it is a _____. *(page 39)*

   1. Small children do not know the difference between what? *(page 39)*

      A _____ and a _____

   2. What words does God hold us accountable for? *(page 39)*

      _____

   3. Read: *"And let the peace (soul harmony which comes) from Christ rule (act as umpire continually) in your hearts [deciding and settling with finality all questions that arise in your minds, in that peaceful state] to which as [members of Christ's] one body you were also called [to live]"* Colossians 3:15 AMP.

      This is the basis for this saying: *(page 40)*

      Peace is the _____ for doing the will of God.

For Further Study:

Live the truth – *"But be ye doers of the word, and not hearers only, deceiving your own selves"* James 1:22.
"Therefore to him that knoweth to do good, and doeth it not, to him it is sin" James 4:17.
Giving your word – Proverbs 6:1-5
Idle words – *"But I say unto you, That every idle word that men shall speak, they shall give account thereof in the day of judgment"* Matthew 12:36.
Integrity – *"The just man walketh in his integrity"* Proverbs 20:7.
Cleansed from idle words – *"The curse causeless shall not come"* Proverbs 26:2.
"Who can understand his errors? cleanse thou me from secret faults" Psalm 19:12.
"Search me, O God, and know my heart: try me, and know my thoughts: And see if there be any wicked way in me, and lead me in the way everlasting" Psalm 139:23, 24; Psalm 25:5; Matthew 5:23-24; 1 John 1:9.

F.   Pride is the _____ of sin. *(page 41)*

Pride won't let you humble yourself to admit wrong or even suffer being wronged. *(page 41)*

Write out Proverbs 18:21.

_____

_____

G.   Can Satan "steal" your word?   ___ Yes   ___ No

1.   What does it mean to "wash" your mind with the "water of the Word of God"? *(page 42)*

Read Ephesians 5:26. _____

2.   Great works are built on great words. *(page 42)*   ___ True   ___ False

Practical:
1.   Who is Jesus? Read Hebrews 1:3; 11:3; John 1:1-5.

_____

What do these tell you about Jesus Christ in relation to truth telling and words?

_____

_____

For Further Study:

Recognizing wrong doing – *"And the men … asked not counsel at the mouth of the Lord"* Joshua 9:14.
"A fool thinks he needs no advice" Proverbs 12:15 TLB.
"It is a badge of honor to accept valid criticism" Proverbs 25:12 TLB. Renew your mind – *"Lie not … seeing that ye have put off the old man … And have put on the new man"* Colossians 3:9, 10.
"And be not conformed to this world: but be ye transformed by the renewing of your mind, that ye may prove what is that good, and acceptable, and perfect, will of God" Romans 12:2.
How to build great works – *"A good man out of the good treasure of his heart bringeth forth that which is good"* Luke 6:45; Hebrews 1:3; 11:3.
Aspire to be a man of your word – *"For in many things we offend all. If any man offend not in word, the same is a perfect man, and able also to bridle the whole body"* James 3:2.

2.   Read Judges 11:30-35 and Proverbs 6:1-3.

What should you do if you've given your word hastily? *(page 39)*

_____

_____

Repeat this prayer out loud:

Father, in the Name of Jesus, I repent of every idle word. Please bring back to my memory the vows I've made that have become a curse to me — vows to do something good, or to do something bad or even to kill myself. I commit to repent of each one as You bring it back to my memory. Please help me learn to watch over my words and immerse myself in Your Word for the "washing" of my mind. Let my name become a name of uprightness and integrity, honesty and truthfulness, even as Your Name is. Amen.

Principles I want to memorize:

Self Test *Lesson 3*

1. A man's name is only as good as his _____.

2. God never gives authority without: *(circle one)*

    a. mercy

    b. salvation

    c. accountability

3. A man's word is the expression of his _____.

4. Circle the three main evidences of a changed life in conversion.

    a. a love for God

    b. a desire for hours of prayer

    c. a burden for world missions

    d. a love for the Word

    e. a love of the brethren

5. The only place where men who love truth will be popular is _____

    _____.

6. To small children, what is the difference between a broken promise and a lie from their father?

    _____

7. What acts as an "umpire" for doing the will of God? _____

8. God's Word says that we will be judged for what words? _____

9. What are great works built on? _____

Keep this test for your own records

Lesson 4
A Covenant Word in Marriage

Lesson 4
A Covenant Word in Marriage

A. Read aloud the following:

"Not a word from their mouth can be trusted" Psalm 5:9 NIV.

"A false witness must be punished; an honest witness is safe" Proverbs 21:28 TLB.

1. In relation to trust, complete these sentences: *(page 44)*

    a. A woman is able to _____ if she can trust his word.

    b. _____ is extended to the limit of _____.

    c. _____ makes _____ possible.

2. Write out James 3:2.

    _____

    _____

    _____

    In relation to trust, what does this verse mean?

    _____

For Further Study:
Trust makes vulnerability possible – *"A trustworthy man keeps a secret"* Proverbs 11:13 NIV.
"Husbands, love your wives, even as Christ also loved the church, and gave himself for it" Ephesians 5:25.

3.   Look up and read aloud Malachi 2:14-15.

4.   **In your own words,** write what the vows of marriage mean. *(pages 44-45)*

   _____

   _____

B.   Every principle in human life emanates from, is originated in or is initiated by _____

   _____. *(page 45)*

   1.   List the three evidences of love. *(page 45)*

      a.   _____

      b.   _____

      c.   _____

   2.   **In your own words,** how can you be sure that God loves you? *(pages 45-46)*

   _____

For Further Study:

Check-up for husbands – *"Husbands, love your wives and do not be harsh with them"* Colossians 3:19 NIV.
Evidences of love – *"Love is … never haughty or selfish or rude. Love does not demand its own way"*
1 Corinthians 13:4, 5 TLB; *"If you love someone you will … always believe in him, always expect the best of him, and always stand your ground in defending him"* 1 Corinthians 13:7 TLB; *"May they be brought to complete unity to let the world know that you sent me and have loved them even as you have loved me"* John 17:23 NIV.
Selflessness of the Trinity – *"For he dwelleth with you, and shall be in you"* John 14:16-17; *"But God commendeth his love toward us, in that, while we were yet sinners, Christ died for us"* Romans 5:8; *"And walk in love, as Christ also hath loved us, and hath given himself for us an offering and a sacrifice to God for a sweetsmelling savour"* Ephesians 5:2.
God's desire to benefit us – *"No good thing will he withhold from them that walk uprightly"* Psalm 84:11. *"He that spared not his own Son, but delivered him up for us all, how shall he not with him also freely give us all things?"* Romans 8:32.

C. Love seeks to benefit others at the expense of _____, while lust seeks to benefit self at the expense of _____. *(page 46)*

    1. Name the three provisions of love. *(page 46)*

       a. _____   b. _____   c. _____

    2. Name three things a man should provide a woman in marriage. *(pages 46-47)*

       a. _____   b. _____   c. _____

    3. A woman's security is NOT primarily found in her home. *(page 47)*   ___ True ___ False

    4. Name at least two ways women react to men's instability. *(page 47)* _____

       _____

    5. Stability in the man's character translates to what in his children? *(page 48)* _____

    6. Name a primary source of a child's security. *(page 48)* _____

       _____

    Look up and read aloud Psalm 112:1-2 and Proverbs 20:7.

For Further Study:

God's desire for intimacy – John 17:21; *"But as many as received him, to them gave he power to become the sons of God, even to them that believe on his name"* John 1:12.

Christ's provisions mirror ours – *"Love your wives, even as Christ also loved the church"* Ephesians 5:25.

Identity – Isaiah 62:12; *"Behold, what manner of love the Father hath bestowed upon us, that we should be called the sons of God"* 1 John 3:1.

A husband's provision for his wife's submission – Ephesians 5:22; *"So ought men to love their wives as their own bodies. He that loveth his wife loveth himself"* Ephesians 5:28.

Security – Genesis 2:24; Proverbs 18:10; Mark 10:9

Stability – *"I have set the Lord always before me. Because he is at my right hand, I shall not be shaken"* Psalm 16:8 NIV; *"He only is my rock and my salvation; he is my defence; I shall not be greatly moved"* Psalm 62:2.

Children blessed by fathers – Psalm 112:1, 2; Proverbs 20:7

"Reverence for God gives a man deep strength; his children have a place of refuge and security" Proverbs 14:26 TLB.

D.   Great men are known by: *(circle one)* *(page 48)*

The great things they built

How rich they became

The greatness of their words

1.   God's Word, sown into the heart of a man, produces what? *(page 48)* _____

2.   Think it over: What kinds of words have you sown into the hearts of people around you?

What kinds of "fruits" have you seen as the result of the words sown?

_____

If you change your words, will it change the "fruits" you see in others?   ___ Yes ___ No

E.   What is the main reason we can allow ourselves to fully love God? *(page 50)*

_____

For Further Study:

The power of words – *"The tongue has the power of life and death, and those who love it will eat its fruit"* Proverbs 18:21 NIV; Psalm 15:2, 3; James 3:9; *"The words of the wise soothe and heal"* Proverbs 12:18 TLB; *"Gentle words cause life and health; griping brings discouragement"* Proverbs 15:4 TLB; *"Evil words destroy. Godly skill rebuilds"* Proverbs 11:9 TLB; *"Anxious hearts are very heavy but a word of encouragement does wonders!"* Proverbs 12:25 TLB; Matthew 12:37; *"He that keepeth his mouth keepeth his life: but he that openeth wide his lips shall have destruction"* Proverbs 13:3; Psalm 119:130; Proverbs 6:2; 12:6; Romans 16:18.
As long as a man's words live, he lives – *"There is living truth in what a good man says"* Proverbs 10:11 TLB.
God's Words sown into a life – *"It is the spirit that quickeneth; the flesh profiteth nothing: the words that I speak unto you, they are spirit, and they are life"* John 6:63; 1 Peter 1:23.
Man's words sown into a life – Proverbs 15:4; *"Godly men are growing a tree that bears life-giving fruit"* Proverbs 11:30 TLB.

1. Name four things required to love a woman as Christ loves the Church. *(page 50)*

    a. _____   c. _____

    b. _____   d. _____

2. Name some rewards for obeying God and accepting responsibility. *(page 50)*

    _____

F. A man of God: *(page 51)*

    1. _____ the woman God gives him as Christ _____.

    2. _____ his family in truth by _____.

    3. _____ in marriage and keeps it, however difficult it is at times.

Practical:

1. Read about the evidences of God's love in John 14:16-17; Romans 5:8; Ephesians 5:2.

    According to these verses, if you were truly loving, what would you no longer do? What would you do?

    _____

    _____

For Further Study:

Love and trust – *"For the king trusts in the Lord; through the unfailing love of the Most High he will not be shaken"* Psalm 21:7 NIV; 1 John 4:10.

Prepare for marriage – *"For which of you, intending to build a tower, sitteth not down first, and counteth the cost, whether he have sufficient to finish it?"* Luke 14:28.

Prepare to love – *"Beloved, if God so loved us, we ought also to love one another ... If we love one another, God dwelleth in us, and his love is perfected in us"* 1 John 4:11, 12; John 15:12, 13.

Prepare your name to have a good character – *"A good name is rather to be chosen than great riches, and loving favour rather than silver and gold"* Proverbs 22:1.

Keep your word in marriage – *"Do you want a long, good life? Then watch your tongue! Keep your lips from lying"* Psalm 34:12, 13 TLB.

2. Take a moment to be brutally honest with yourself. What would/does marriage provide?

Identity: _____

Security: _____

Stability: _____

Repeat this prayer out loud:

Father, in Jesus' Name, I have never realized how unloving I am, and I want to change! I repent of every unloving word I've ever spoken, every unloving action I've ever taken. Please help me to be the kind of man that would make my family proud to carry my name. I commit to provide a home that is full of peace and security. Thank You, Lord, for helping me to start today. Amen.

For Further Study:

A man of God loves his wife – Ephesians 5:25.

A man of God leads his family in truth by keeping his word – Proverbs 11:3; 20:7.

A man of God gives his word in marriage and keeps it, no matter how difficult – *"Therefore guard your passions! Keep faith with the wife of your youth. For the Lord, the God of Israel, says he hates divorce and cruel men. Therefore control your passions – let there be no divorcing of your wives"* Malachi 2:15-16 TLB.

The family of a man of God can depend on him – *"A faithful man shall abound with blessings"* Proverbs 28:20.

Self Test *Lesson 4*

1. A woman should be able to trust a man, even when he doesn't keep his word.   ___ True   ___ False

2. What makes vulnerability in a marriage possible? _____

3. From where does every principle in human life emanate?

   _____

4. What are the evidences of love?

   a. _____

   b. _____

   c. _____

5. What are the provisions of love?

   a. _____   b. _____   c. _____

6. Love desires to benefit others _____.

7. In what area is a woman's security primarily found?

   _____

8. A man should "count the cost" before entering into marriage.   ___ True   ___ False

9. Great men are known by the greatness of their _____.

10. Stability in a man's character translates to _____ in his children.

Keep this test for your own records

Word, Gesture, Spirit & Taking Action

Lesson 5
Word, Gesture, Spirit & Taking Action

I. **Word, Gesture, Spirit (Chapter 6)**

A. Mark "T" for True and "F" for False. *(pages 55-57)*

_____ "Living by faith" without regular income is a naturally exciting life to any woman.

_____ Shared prayer is crucial to a marriage.

_____ Ministers should always put ministry ahead of marriage.

_____ Rejection is the hardest thing for a man to take.

_____ Winning back a woman's love requires courtship all over again.

_____ Jesus promised to save only your soul. Everything else is up to you.

_____ God doesn't just save us *FROM* sin; He saves us *TO* righteousness.

B. List the three methods of communication. *(page 58)*

_____   _____   _____

1. Is the old axiom "actions speak louder than words" true? *(page 58)* ___ Yes ___ No

---

For Further Study:

Words are visible expressions of what is in the heart – *"A good man out of the good treasure of his heart bringeth forth that which is good; and an evil man out of the evil treasure of his heart bringeth forth that which is evil: for of the abundance of the heart his mouth speaketh"* Luke 6:45; Proverbs 10:20; 32.

Gestures confirm the words – *"Little children, let us stop just saying we love people; let us really love them, and show it by our actions"* 1 John 3:18 TLB; Matthew 7:21; 21:28-31; Titus 1:16; *"Dear brothers, what's the use of saying that you have faith and are Christians if you aren't proving it by helping others? Will that kind of faith save anyone?"* James 2:14 TLB.

2.   Does communication by "spirit" show up in attitude? *(page 58)* ___ Yes ___ No

3.   How does the best communication by "spirit" happen? *(page 58)* _____

4.   Look up and read aloud Luke 6:45.

5.   Read aloud: *"An unreliable messenger can cause a lot of trouble. Reliable communication permits progress"* Proverbs 13:17 TLB. In what ways have you experienced this?

_____

_____

_____

6.   What does sin always cause? *(page 59)* _____

7.   What happens when communication stops? *(page 60)* _____

_____

8.   For a husband, communication includes _____ to his wife. *(page 61)*

9.   For a father, communication includes _____ to his children. *(page 61)*

For Further Study:

Communication by spirit – *"For as he thinketh in his heart, so is he: Eat and drink, saith he to thee; but his heart is not with thee"* Proverbs 23:7; *"A man with hate in his heart may sound pleasant enough, but don't believe him; for he is cursing you in his heart. Though he pretends to be so kind, his hatred will finally come to light for all to see"* Proverbs 26:24-26 TLB.

Prayer produces intimacy, for example – *"They joined with the other believers in regular attendance at ... prayer meetings ... And all the believers ... shared everything with each other"* Acts 2:42-44 TLB.

Reliable communication – Mark 4:11-12, 23-24

Distortion in the hearers – *"Then a voice spoke from heaven saying, 'I have already done this, and I will do it again.' When the crowd heard the voice, some of them thought it was thunder"* John 12:28-29 TLB.

Deliberate distortion – *"And they will deceive every one his neighbour, and will not speak the truth: they have taught their tongue to speak lies, and weary themselves to commit iniquity"* Jeremiah 9:5; Romans 16:18.

C. The formula for success in a man's life is: *(page 61)*

_____   _____   _____

Write out James 1:19, 20.

_____

_____

_____

_____

II. **Taking Action (Chapter 7)**

A. Name at least one way a man can communicate by gesture. *(page 65)* _____

B. Write out 1 John 3:16.

_____

_____

_____

For Further Study:

Sin distorts – *"For the wages of sin is death"* Romans 6:23; Ezekiel 18:4; Romans 1:21; 1 John 1:6.

Flesh distorts – *"Any story sounds true until someone tells the other side and sets the record straight"* Proverbs 18:17 TLB.

Prevent distortion – 1 Peter 3:12; 1 John 1:7; 3:21.

The ultimate abnormality – Proverbs 29:18; Hosea 4:6, 14; Amos 8:11; Malachi 2:13-16

Rules for communication – With others – *"Wherefore, my beloved brethren, let every man be swift to hear, slow to speak, slow to wrath"* James 1:19; With wives – *"Husbands, in the same way be considerate as you live with your wives, and treat them with respect"* 1 Peter 3:7 NIV; With children – *"And, ye fathers, provoke not your children to wrath: but bring them up in the nurture and admonition of the Lord"* Ephesians 6:4.

Communicate your love – *"Open rebuke is better than hidden love!"* Proverbs 27:5 TLB; *"Let us not love in word, neither in tongue; but in deed and in truth"* 1 John 3:18.

1. Read: *"Not everyone that saith unto me, Lord, Lord, shall enter into the kingdom of heaven; but he that doeth the will of my Father which is in heaven"* Matthew 7:21.

2. Words alone don't satisfy — _____ do. *(page 65)*

3. List some ways you can "lay down your life" with gestures and actions. _____

    _____

C. Gestures are commonly known in life as communication tools and indicators. *(page 66)*

1. Lovers speak volumes with _____.

2. Parents can control their children with _____.

3. Husbands say it with _____.

4. The greatest gesture of love known to mankind was:

    _____

D. Gesture is the confirmation of the _____. *(page 67)*

For Further Study:

Gestures communicate – *"They profess that they know God; but in works they deny him"* Titus 1:16; Proverbs 27:14.

Gestures satisfy – *"If you have a friend who is in need of food and clothing, and you say to him, 'Well, good-bye and God bless you; stay warm and eat hearty,' and then don't give him clothes or food, what good does that do?"* James 2:15, 16 TLB; *"For I was an hungered, and ye gave me meat: I was thirsty, and ye gave me drink: I was a stranger, and ye took me in: Naked, and ye clothed me: I was sick, and ye visited me: I was in prison, and ye came unto me"* Matthew 25:35.

Gestures prove love for God – Matthew 7:21: *"If anyone has material possessions and sees his brother in need but has no pity on him, how can the love of God be in him?"* 1 John 3:17 NIV.

God's ultimate gesture – John 3:16

1. Write out James 2:17.

   _____

   _____

2. Circle the letter of the true statements. *(pages 68-69)*

   a. Emotional deprivation can occur in "normal" families.

   b. If people are cared for physically, they don't need emotional gestures.

   c. Men must learn to show affection by gesture.

   d. Many men are unable to love or be loved normally because of the lack of affection and attention in their own childhood.

3. A problem in homes today is that many men don't know how to communicate: *(circle one) (page 69)*

   a. about sports   b. during meals   c. love

Practical:

1. Read Proverbs 23:7; 1 John 3:18.

   With what gestures can you communicate God's love to others this week?

   At work: _____

   To your wife: _____

For Further Study:

Gestures confirm the Word – James 2:17; *"My message and my preaching were not with wise and persuasive words, but with a demonstration of the Spirit's power"* 1 Corinthians 2:4 NIV; Proverbs 27:5; James 1:14; 1 John 3:18.

Gestures of gratitude – *"Don't worry about anything; instead, pray about everything; tell God your needs and don't forget to thank him for his answers"* Philippians 4:6 TLB.

"It is a good thing to give thanks unto the Lord" Psalm 92:1.

Give your family a gesture of love today – *"Now I want you to be leaders also in the spirit of cheerful giving ... This is one way to prove that your love is real, that it goes beyond mere words"* 2 Corinthians 8:7, 8 TLB.

With your children:

_____

For your pastor and church:

_____

2.   Have you ever had a "father's hug"? Where can you get one this week?

_____

_____

3.   Read: *"Now I want you to be leaders also in the spirit of cheerful giving … This is one way to prove that your love is real, that it goes beyond mere words"* 2 Corinthians 8:7-8 TLB.

Rephrase this **in your own words.** _____

_____

Repeat this prayer out loud:

Father, You acted on Your love for me, by sending Christ to die for me, while I was still lost in sin. Help me to be quick to love and to show my love, not just talk about it. Your love is constant; help mine to be also. Forgive me for having an ungrateful heart at times. I determine to be a man who offers up praise, not only to You, but to my family. Thank You, in Jesus' Name. Amen.

Principles I want to memorize:

Self Test *Lesson 5*

1. Praying together is one of the best means of good marital communication.   ___ True ___ False

2. Winning back a woman's love requires courtship all over again.   ___ True ___ False

3. God doesn't just save us *FROM* sin; He saves us *TO* righteousness.   ___ True ___ False

4. List the three major ways by which we communicate.

    a. _____

    b. _____

    c. _____

5. The Bible says, *"Reliable communication permits* _____*."*

6. When communication stops, _____ sets in.

7. The greatest gesture of love ever made to mankind was what? _____

8. It is absolutely essential that men learn to show their affection by gesture, no matter how difficult it may seem for them. What are some ways you can communicate love by gesture?

    a. _____

    b. _____

    c. _____

    d. _____

9. A man must support his words by his _____.

Keep this test for your own records

Lesson 6
Spirit to Spirit & The Sacredness of Sex

Lesson 6
Spirit to Spirit & The Sacredness of Sex

I. **Spirit to Spirit (Chapter 8)**

    A. Prayer produces _____. *(page 72)*

        1. Men should read from the book of _____ in the morning. *(page 72)*

        2. Men should read from the book of _____ in the evening. *(page 72)*

        3. Communicating spirit to spirit is the most _____ form of communication possible. *(page 72)*

        4. Men glorify God by loving their wives. *(page 73)* ___ True ___ False

    B. Every word we speak releases the _____ in which it is spoken. *(page 73)*

        1. Write out John 6:63. _____

                _____

        2. Write out Romans 8:16. _____

                _____

For Further Study:
Communication by spirit – Luke 5:22; *"And immediately when Jesus perceived in his spirit that they so reasoned within themselves, he said unto them, Why reason ye these things in your hearts?"* Mark 2:8.

The Word releases the spirit – *"For as he thinketh in his heart, so is he: Eat and drink, saith he to thee; but his heart is not with thee"* Proverbs 23:7.

Intimate communication – *"We have spoken freely to you, Corinthians, and opened wide our hearts to you. We are not withholding affection from you"* 2 Corinthians 6:11, 12 NIV; 1 Corinthians 2:11.

Forgiveness is in word and spirit – *"This is how my heavenly Father will treat each of you unless you forgive your brother from your heart"* Matthew 18:35 NIV; Psalm 49:7, 8; Ephesians 1:7; 2:8-9.

C. **In your own words,** what does it mean that people "broadcast" their spirits? *(page 77)*

_____

_____

1. What are some "spiritual" influences that surround you every day?

    Positive: a. _____ b. _____ c. _____

    Negative: a. _____ b. _____ c. _____

2. What must men do to create a bulwark against influencing spirits? *(page 77)*

    a. _____

    b. _____

D. When a man changes, what can he expect at home? *(page 80)* _____

1. A man's heart determines his speech, but what determines his affection? *(page 80)*

    a. his feelings   b. his actions   c. other people's reactions to him

2. If you want to change your emotions, change your _____. *(page 80)*

For Further Study:

Guard your heart – *"Above all else, guard your heart, for it is the wellspring of life"* Proverbs 4:23 NIV; *"Casting down imaginations, and every high thing that exalteth itself against the knowledge of God, and bringing into captivity every thought to the obedience of Christ"* 2 Corinthians 10:5; *"Since we have these promises, dear friends, let us purify ourselves from everything that contaminates body and spirit, perfecting holiness out of reverence for God"* 2 Corinthians 7:1 NIV; *"But those things which proceed out of the mouth come forth from the heart; and they defile a man"* Matthew 15:18.

God wants to be glorified in marriage – Ephesians 5:25; *"Whatsoever you do, do all to the glory of God"* 1 Corinthians 10:31; Matthew 5:16; *"Christ in you, the hope of glory"* Colossians 1:27.

Jesus revealed the Father to us – John 10:37; 12:49; 14:7, 10.

Our actions confirm our words and determine our emotions – Psalm 126:5; Matthew 15:18; Luke 6:45; 2 Corinthians 7:1; 2 Timothy 2:21; *"Let us not be weary in well doing: for in due season we shall reap, if we faint not"* Galatians 6:9; Hosea 10:12.

3.   Emotions follow _____. *(page 80)*

4.   A man's love without _____ is meaningless. *(page 81)*

II.   **The Sacredness of Sex (Chapter 9)**

A.   Men are to be _____ when they marry. *(page 86)*

in love   virgins   experienced

1.   Men are to be _____ after marriage. *(page 86)*

faithful   the sole source of family support   less happy

2.   Real men respond to _____ when they hear it. *(page 86)*

sports scores   a joke   truth

3.   Sex is _____. *(page 86)*

dirty   sacred   not to be talked about

4.   _____ must teach the truth about sex. *(page 87)*

Schools   Television   The Church

For Further Study:

Cleanse your spirit – *"Wherewithall shall a young man cleanse his way? by taking heed thereto according to thy word"* Psalm 119:9; John 17:17; *"You are already clean because of the word I have spoken to you"* John 15:3 NIV. Communicate freely – *"A good man out of the good treasure of the heart bringeth forth good things"* Matthew 12:35; Luke 6:45; 1 John 3:18.
God's love without Calvary would be meaningless – *"But God demonstrates his own love for us in this: While we were still sinners, Christ died for us"* Romans 5:8 NIV.
The world has perverted sex – Romans 1:24. The Church must correct the perversion – Malachi 2:7.
Sex is honorable – Hebrews 13:4; *"Every good gift and every perfect gift is from above, and cometh down from the Father of lights, with whom is no variableness, neither shadow of turning"* James 1:17.
God's covenant plan – Genesis 17:10; Romans 2:29; 4:3

B.   Sex is the highest physical act of love between two people, _____

_____, which is a covenant relationship. *(page 87)*

1.   Circumcision was an _____ evidence of an _____ work. *(page 88)*

2.   Circumcision was of the _____ first and of the flesh _____. *(page 88)*

3.   A blood sacrifice represents cutting off uncleanness. *(page 89)*   ___ True ___ False

C.   What became the sign of the new covenant relationship? *(page 90)* _____

1.   Baptism is an act of identification with Christ. *(page 90)*   ___ True ___ False

2.   God called us to live a crucified life, dead and boring. *(page 90)*   ___ True ___ False

3.   Water baptism is an _____ evidence of an _____ work. *(page 91)*

4.   Read 1 Peter 3:21-22.

D.   Sex is also an _____ evidence of an _____ work. *(page 91)*

For Further Study:

Circumcision was of the heart first – *"Circumcise yourselves to the Lord, and take away the foreskins of your heart"* Jeremiah 4:4; *"In whom also ye are circumcised with the circumcision made without hands, in putting off the body of the sins of the flesh by the circumcision of Christ"* Colossians 2:11; Genesis 17; 11; Leviticus 17:11; Matthew 26:28.

Water baptism – Romans 6:3; Colossians 2:12; *"For as many of you as have been baptized into Christ have put on Christ"* Galatians 3:27; *"He that believeth and is baptized shall be saved"* Mark 16:16.

Marriage is a covenant – *"Therefore shall a man leave his father and his mother, and shall cleave unto his wife: and they shall be one flesh"* Genesis 2:24; *"You were united to your wife by the Lord. In God's wise plan, when you married, the two of you became one person in his sight"* Malachi 2:15 TLB; Romans 7:2.

1. Marriage is a covenant relationship. *(page 91)*   ___ True   ___ False

2. Sex was made for loving and giving. *(page 91)*   ___ True   ___ False

3. Sex came from the devil. *(page 92)*   ___ True   ___ False

4. God creates; Satan counterfeits. *(page 92)*   ___ True   ___ False

Practical:

1. Read and meditate on Ephesians 5:25-32.

2. Name other body parts that the Bible says need "circumcision." *(pages 88-89)*

_____

What does that mean?

_____

_____

For Further Study:

The marriage covenant – *"Yet is she thy companion, and the wife of thy covenant"* Malachi 2:14; *"The man should give his wife all that is her right as a married woman, and the wife should do the same for the husband"* 1 Corinthians 7:3 TLB; *"Keep faith with the wife of your youth"* Malachi 2:15 TLB; *"Honor your marriage and its vows, and be pure; for God will surely punish all those who are immoral or commit adultery"* Hebrews 13:4 TLB. Love, not lust – John 10:10; 15:13; 1 Corinthians 13:5; Ephesians 5:25; 2 Timothy 3:2; Hebrews 13:4; James 4:1-3

3. Read Hebrews 13:4. Explain it **in your own words**.

_____

_____

Repeat this prayer out loud:

Father, thank You for teaching me the riches of Your Word, for showing me what these things mean. Today I take every thought in my mind captive and surrender it to Jesus Christ. I cut off impure thoughts and feelings that are betraying me into the hands of the devil. And I take on Your Word as my shield, my standard and my rule of conduct. Thank You for this opportunity, Lord! Amen.

For Further Study:

Additional references on spiritual influences – *"He who walks with the wise grows wise, but a companion of fools suffers harm"* Proverbs 13:20 NIV; *"And lead us not into temptation, but deliver us from evil"* Matthew 6:13; *"Watch and pray, that ye enter not into temptation: the spirit indeed is willing, but the flesh is weak"* Matthew 26:41; *"What comes out of a man is what makes him 'unclean.' For from within, out of men's hearts, come evil thoughts, sexual immorality, theft, murder, adultery, greed, malice, deceit, lewdness, envy, slander, arrogance and folly. All these evils come from inside and make a man 'unclean'"* Mark 7:20-23 NIV; *"Do not be misled: 'Bad company corrupts good character'"* 1 Corinthians 15:33; *"For we wrestle not against flesh and blood, but against principalities, against powers, against the rulers of the darkness of this world, against spiritual wickedness in high places"* Ephesians 6:12; *"Run from anything that gives you the evil thoughts that young men often have, but stay close to anything that makes you want to do right"* 2 Timothy 2:22 TLB; *"Be sober, be vigilant; because your adversary the devil, as a roaring lion, walketh about, seeking whom he may devour"* 1 Peter 5:8.

Self Test *Lesson 6*

1. _____ produces intimacy.

2. Every word we speak releases the _____ in which it is spoken.

3. If you want to change your emotions, change your _____.

4. **In your own words,** write out a definition of what circumcision represents.

   _____

   _____

   _____

5. What is the sign of our new covenant relationship with God? _____

6. God has called us to live a "resurrected" life!   ___ True ___ False

7. Sex is an external evidence of an _____.

8. Lust desires to gratify self at the expense of _____.

9. Love desires to benefit others even at the expense of _____.

10. Any sex outside of marriage is _____.

Lesson 7
The Glory of Virginity

Lesson 7
The Glory of Virginity

A.   Read Deuteronomy 22:13-21.

Write the letter of the word next to the statement it completes. *(pages 93-96)*

a. virgins   b. slander   c. glory   d. word   e. death

_____ 1. Virginity is a _____ to both men and women.

_____ 2. God expects both men and women to be _____ when they marry.

_____ 3. The Old Testament penalty for a woman defrauding her spouse about virginity was _____.

_____ 4. The man's virginity cannot be proven, because he is to be taken at his _____.

_____ 5. There is a penalty for men who _____ a woman.

B.   Write out Ephesians 5:31-32. _____

_____

_____

_____

C.   Read Psalm 101:5.

If you are guilty of having slandered a woman's virtue, you must: *(page 96)*

1.   _____   2. _____

For Further Study:
Stay pure – Proverbs 6:23; *"It is God's will that you should be sanctified: that you should avoid sexual immorality; that each of you should learn to control his own body in a way that is holy and honorable"* 1 Thessalonians 4:3, 4 NIV; Proverbs 5:8, 9; Malachi 2:15.
The purpose of punishing sexual fraud – *"So thou shalt put away evil from among you"* Deuteronomy 22:24.

D. **In your own words,** what is the "fear of the Lord"? *(page 97)*

_____

_____

1. Write out Acts 9:31.

_____

_____

2. What is the "beginning of wisdom"? *(circle one) (page 97)*

   a. the fear of the Lord   b. this curriculum   c. prayer

3. What is the balance to the "comfort of the Holy Ghost"? *(circle one) (page 97)*

   a. living in condemnation   b. the fear of the Lord   c. the guidance of the Word

4. Read Ephesians 4:19-24. What is the definition of the word "lasciviousness"? *(page 97)*

   _____

5. The rise and fall of the fear of the Lord in the life of believers has a direct bearing on the rise and

   fall of unrighteousness in a community or nation. *(page 97)*   ___ True ___ False

For Further Study:

The fear of the Lord – *"The fear of the Lord is the beginning of wisdom"* Proverbs 9:10; *"By the fear of the Lord men depart from evil"* Proverbs 16:6; *"Then had the churches rest throughout all Judea and Galilee and Samaria, and were edified; and walking the fear of the Lord, and in the comfort of the Holy Ghost, were multiplied"* Acts 9:31; John 16:8.

Conviction of sin within the Church – *"But the face of the Lord is against them that do evil"* 1 Peter 3:12; *"Righteousness exalteth a nation: but sin is a reproach to any people"* Proverbs 14:34; *"Ye are the light of the world. A city that is set on a hill cannot be hid"* Matthew 5:14; *"If therefore the light that is in thee be darkness, how great is that darkness!"* Matthew 6:23; *"By the blessing of the upright the city is exalted: but it is overthrown by the mouth of the wicked"* Proverbs 11:11.

E.   Public denunciation of sin is dependent on: *(circle one)* *(page 98)*

a. private renunciation   b. good laws   c. boldness

1.   Every man who renounces sin makes an impact on the world around him. *(page 98)*

___ True ___ False

2.   What is the major reason God wanted Israel to walk in the fear of the Lord? *(page 98)*

_____

_____

F.   On the wedding night, a couple's first act of sexual intimacy causes the shedding of blood, which is what

sign? *(page 99)* _____

1.   Read Romans 12:1. What is "reasonable" about keeping one's virginity until marriage? *(page 100)*

_____

2.   God is calling you to: *(circle one)* *(page 100)*

a. a dull life   b. live an impossible lifestyle   c. excellence

G.   Once you've lost your virginity, there's nothing else you can do about it. *(page 101)*

___ True ___ False

For Further Study:

Private renunciation of sin – *"If I regard iniquity in my heart, the Lord will not hear me"* Psalm 66:18;
Romans 2:21-24; *"Thou shalt keep the commandments of the Lord thy God, and walk in his ways. And all
people of the earth shall see that thou art called by the name of the Lord; and they shall be afraid of thee"*
Deuteronomy 28:9, 10; *"Wherefore come out from among them, and be ye separate, saith the Lord, and touch not
the unclean thing; and I will receive you"* 2 Corinthians 6:17.
The covenant of marriage – Malachi 2:14; Romans 12:1; *"The husband's body does not belong to him alone but
also to his wife"* 1 Corinthians 7:4 NIV.
Restoration of virginity – *"And I will restore you the years that the locust hath eaten, the cankerworm, and the
caterpiller, and the palmerworm"* Joel 2:25.

1. While you cannot physically get back your virginity, you can receive it again ... *(page 101)*

   _____

2. If you are married, your attitude toward your marriage bed can be ... *(page 101)*

   _____

   _____

Practical:

1. Read: *"You speak continually against your brother and slander your own mother's son. These things you have done and I kept silent; you thought I was altogether like you. But I will rebuke you and accuse you to your face. Consider this, you who forget God, or I will tear you to pieces, with none to rescue"* Psalm 50:20-22 NIV.

   List women whom you may have slandered and repent of it, even to them, if needed.

   _____

2. If you are married, prayerfully read this chapter again with your spouse, and ask God to correct anything you've done wrong — if you started wrong, or have been wrong — and ask Him to give you intimacy that is a glory to Him.

Repeat this prayer out loud:

Father, in the Name of Jesus, I repent of all past sexual sins. I present my body, holy, acceptable to You, which is my reasonable service. By faith, I receive the Holy Spirit's power in my life to renew within me the spirit and the glory of virginity. In the spirit of virginity, I present my body, holy and acceptable, to that person to whom I will marry (or to whom I am married). I accept Your provision for this covenant relationship in my life and thank You for it. Amen.

Principles I want to memorize:

Self Test *Lesson 7*

1. To God and the godly, virginity is a _____.

2. God does not demand that a man be a virgin when he marries.   ___ True ___ False

3. It is not possible to prove the virginity of a man. The man's _____ was to be reliable.

4. What is the meaning of the word "lasciviousness"? _____

5. The way you live as an individual does not have much effect on this world.   ___ True ___ False

6. Why did God want Israel to walk in the fear of the Lord?

   _____

7. What is the result of a man who renounces sin?

   _____

8. When a husband and wife have their first time of sexual intimacy, it is a sign before God that they have

   entered into a _____.

9. You cannot receive your virginity again physically, but you can receive it again spiritually.

   ___ True ___ False

Keep this test for your own records

Lesson 8
The Principle of Release &
God Made Sex Good

Lesson 8
The Principle of Release & God Made Sex Good

I. **The Principle of Release (Chapter 11)**

   A. Read out loud: *"Receive ye the Holy Ghost: Whose soever sins ye remit, they are remitted unto them; and whose soever sins ye retain, they are retained"* John 20:22-23.

   1. When you forgive anyone his sins, you _____. *(page 104)*

   2. When you do not forgive, you _____ the sin to you. *(page 104)*

   3. Why do men often make the same mistakes with their sons that their fathers made with them?

      (page 104) _____

   4. List some things that create a "wall" that keep us from forgiving. *(page 105)*

   _____

   B. Negative sexual experiences will eventually just fade away. *(page 107)* ___ True ___ False

   1. Men have also been victimized and sexually abused. *(page 108)* ___ True ___ False

   2. To forgive as God forgives, _____. *(page 109)*

   3. What can you do if you have attitudes about sex that are not based on the Word of God? *(page 109)*

   _____

   4. God wants us free, unencumbered to live for Him. *(page 109)* ___ True ___ False

For Further Study:

Sins passed through generations – Exodus 34:7; *"Watch out that no bitterness takes root among you, for as it springs up it causes deep trouble, hurting many in their spiritual lives"* Hebrews 12:15. God's provision for removal of sin – *"As far as the east is from the west, so far hath he removed our transgressions from us"* Psalm 103:12; *"And when ye stand praying, forgive, if ye have ought against any: that your Father also which is in heaven may forgive you your trespasses"* Mark 11:25; Isaiah 10:27; Zechariah 4:6.

II. **God Made Sex Good** (Chapter 12)

A. List at least one reason why God made sex good. *(page 112)* _____

_____

1. Circle everything that sex is. *(page 112)*
    a. something to be ashamed of
    b. lovely
    c. good
    d. unholy
    e. decent
    f. something to avoid
    g. to be secretly lusted after
    h. something in keeping with the covenant relationship between man and woman

2. God created the entire earth in the _____. *(page 112)*

3. Man, through sin, recreated earth in the _____. *(page 112)*

4. God creates; Satan counterfeits. *(page 112)*   ___ True   ___ False

5. Sin always promises to _____ and _____, but only desires to

    _____ and _____. *(page 112)*

6. Love is _____; lust is _____. *(page 113)*

7. Lust is a counterfeit for love. *(page 113)*   ___ True   ___ False

---

For Further Study:

Everything God made is good – Genesis 1:31; Psalm 139:14.

Man makes good things negative – Genesis 3:17.

Sin desires to enslave – *"But exhort one another daily, while it is called Today; lest any of you be hardened through the deceitfulness of sin"* Hebrews 3:13.

Receive release – *"For the weapons of our warfare are not carnal, but mighty through God to the pulling down of strongholds; Casting down imaginations, and every high thing that exalteth itself against the knowledge of God, and bringing into captivity every thought to the obedience of Christ"* 2 Corinthians 10:4, 5; Luke 4:18.

B.   Pornography is a substitute for _____. *(page 113)*

    1.   Prayer is designed to produce intimacy. *(page 113)*   ___ True ___ False

    2.   Pornography promises intimacy but produces only distance. Pornography only _____

       and _____. *(page 113)*

    3.   Any man who _____ his wife to engage in sexual acts of _____ is operating out of lust, not love. *(page 114)*

    4.   Write out Romans 14:23b.

    _____

C.   Where does change begin? *(circle one) (page 118)*

when our wives change   in church   with us

    1.   Fill in with the correct words: *(page 118)*

    misunderstanding   strife   impatience   disease

    _____ is the tool of the flesh.

    _____ is the tool of the devil.

For Further Study:

Satan counterfeits – 2 Thessalonians 2:9, 10; *"And no marvel; for Satan himself is transformed into an angel of light"* 2 Corinthians 11:14.

Love, not lust, satisfies – *"The Lord thy God in the midst of thee is mighty ... he will rest in his love"* Zephaniah 3:17; *"From whence come wars and fightings among you? come they not hence, even of your lusts that war in your members?"* James 4:1, 2.

Lust is degenerative – James 1:14, 15; *"But the wicked are like the troubled sea, when it cannot rest, whose waters cast up mire and dirt"* Isaiah 57:20; *"The way of transgressors is hard"* Proverbs 13:15; 2 Samuel 13:1, 13, 15.

Love and sex – *"Love does not demand its own way"* 1 Corinthians 13:5 TLB.

Sexual acts cannot be forced on the spouse – *"For whatsoever is not of faith is sin"* Romans 14:23.

2. The Holy Spirit stays outside the bedroom at night. *(page 119)* ___ True ___ False

3. Read aloud: *"Marriage should be honored by all, and the marriage bed kept pure, for God will judge the adulterer and all the sexually immoral"* Hebrews 13:4 NIV.

4. Women don't battle with lust. *(page 119)* ___ True ___ False

5. Many women struggle due to their husbands' lusts. *(page 119)* ___ True ___ False

D. What is the basic part of communication? *(page 119)* _____

E. You make a success in life because of your ability to speak. *(page 119)* ___ True ___ False

Practical:
1. Whom do you need to forgive for past sexual sins?

    _____

2. What past experiences may have caused you to think wrongly about sex? Ask God to bring them to your remembrance, so you can release them through forgiveness.

Repeat this prayer out loud:

Father, in Jesus' Name, I come to You to receive a healing for my sex life, including my past and my thought life. By faith, I receive Your Spirit, and by the authority of the Word and the ability of Your Spirit, I forgive those who have sinned against me sexually. I also forgive myself for every sexual sin I have committed. I release it out of my life and receive the healing virtue that restores what was taken from me. I now honor You in my marriage bed and my relationship with my wife. Amen.

For Further Study:

Change begins with you – *"Each of us must bear some faults and burdens of his own. For none of us is perfect!"* Galatians 6:5 TLB.
Impatience – *"For ye have need of patience, that, after ye have done the will of God, ye might receive the promise"* Hebrews 10:36.
Misunderstanding – *"For he (Satan) is a liar, and the father of it"* John 8:44.
Never quit – *"And let us not be weary in well-doing: for in due season we shall reap, if we faint not"* Galatians 6:9; *"No, dear brothers, I am still not all I should be but I am bringing all my energies to bear on this one thing: Forgetting the past and looking forward to what lies ahead, I strain to reach the end of the race and receive the prize for which God is calling us up to heaven because of what Christ Jesus did for us"* Philippians 3:13, 14 TLB.

Self Test *Lesson 8*

1. Jesus said that before you are really able to forgive as He forgave, you must first receive

   _____.

2. You retain the sins that you do not release through forgiveness. ___ True ___ False

3. Sons who do not forgive the sins of their fathers often make the same mistakes with their sons.

   ___ True ___ False

4. In creation, God created the whole earth in the _____.

5. Sin promises to _____ and _____, but desires only to _____ and

   _____.

6. Love is insatiable; lust is satisfying. ___ True ___ False

7. What is one substitute for prayer? _____

8. When a man forces his wife to do something contrary to her consecration and coerces her to do something

   outside of faith, it is wrong. ___ True ___ False

9. Where does change begin? _____

10. What is one of the most important ways a man ministers to his wife? _____

Keep this test for your own records

Lesson 9
The Circumcised Marriage &
Master or Servant

Lesson 9
The Circumcised Marriage & Master or Servant

I.   **The Circumcised Marriage (Chapter 13)**

   A.   Mark "T" for True and "F" for False. *(pages 123-124)*

   _____ 1. A successful marriage is based upon friendship, not romance.

   _____ 2. Few marriages ever survive with only "Hollywood" romance.

   _____ 3. A young man needs to become sexually experienced before marriage.

   _____ 4. A young man needs to know how to be a friend to a girl before marriage.

   _____ 5. You can build a life on memories.

   _____ 6. There is a difference between good advice and good news.

   B.   Circumcision represents two things. What are they? *(page 125)*

   1. _____

   2. _____

   C.   Couples must be willing to _____ the past, not resurrect it. *(page 126)*

   live with   talk extensively about   bury

For Further Study:

Circumcision – *"And the Lord thy God will circumcise thine heart, and the heart of thy seed, to love the Lord thy God with all thine heart, and with all thy soul, that thou mayest live"* Deuteronomy 30:6; *"In whom also ye are circumcised with the circumcision made without hands, in putting off the body of the sins of the flesh by the circumcision of Christ"* Colossians 2:11; *"This is my covenant, which ye shall keep, between me and you and thy seed after thee; Every man child among you shall be circumcised"* Genesis 17:10.

Counseling – *"For unto us a child is born, unto us a son is given: and the government shall be upon his shoulder: and his name shall be called wonderful, Counsellor"* Isaiah 9:6; *"It is the Spirit that quickeneth"* John 6:63; *"The words that I speak unto you, they are spirit and they are life"* John 6:63.

Obedience – *"If ye be willing and obedient, ye shall eat the good of the land"* Isaiah 1:19; *"But if anyone keeps looking steadily into God's law for free men, he will not only remember it but he will do what it says, and God will greatly bless him in everything he does"* James 1:25 TLB.

1. Read: *"If they had been thinking with [homesick] remembrance of that country from which they were emigrants, they would have found constant opportunity to return to it"* Hebrews 11:15 AMP.

   How does this relate to our study? _____

2. God can circumcise your heart in marriage, just as He did with your sins when you were saved.

   (page 126) ___ True ___ False

3. God is not a _____. He is a miracle worker. *(page 128)*

II. **Master or Servant (Chapter 14)**

   A. Sex and money are both expressions of love. *(page 131)* ___ True ___ False

   1. The blessing is in the _____, not the _____. *(page 131)*

   2. Name some Biblical examples of people who had issues with money. *(pages 131-132)*

      _____

   3. Having too much money can be a problem, just as having too little is. *(page 132)*

      ___ True ___ False

   4. What is worry? *(page 132)* _____

For Further Study:

God transforms our whole lives with His love – *"Therefore if any man be in Christ, he is a new creature: old things are passed away; behold, all things are become new"* 2 Corinthians 5:17; *"And hope maketh not ashamed; because the love of God is shed abroad in our hearts by the Holy Ghost which is given unto us"* Romans 5:5. Heart change – *"Circumcision is that of the heart, in the spirit, and not in the letter"* Romans 2:29; *"A new heart also will I give you, and a new spirit will I put within you: and I will take away the stony heart out of your flesh, and I will give you an heart of flesh"* Ezekiel 36:26.
Money can bring temptation and worry – *"But they that will be rich fall into temptation and a snare, and into many foolish and hurtful lusts"* Proverbs 15:27; Isaiah 1:23; 1 Timothy 6:9; 2 Peter 2:15; *"The rich man's wealth is his strong city, and as a high wall in his own conceit"* Proverbs 18:11; *"The cares of this world, and the deceitfulness of riches"* Mark 4:19; *"Be anxious for nothing"* Philippians 4:6.

B.   Read out loud Matthew 6:33.

   1.   What makes faith for everything else possible? *(page 132)*

   _____

   2.   I know what is best for myself, and I just need to communicate it to God. *(page 133)*

   ___ True   ___ False

   3.   Describe how men act when their lives are based on circumstances, not faith. *(page 133)*

   _____

   4.   What is the source for issues of the flesh? *(page 134)* _____

   5.   What is a scriptural term for laziness? *(page 134)* _____

For Further Study:

Seek God, not money – "*If … thou shalt seek the Lord thy God, thou shalt find him, if thou seek him with all thy heart and with all thy soul*" Deuteronomy 4:29; "*No man can serve two masters: for either he will hate the one, and love the other; or else he will hold to the one, and despise the other. Ye cannot serve God and mammon*" Matthew 6:24; 6:33; "*Draw nigh to God, and he will draw nigh to you. Cleanse your hands, ye sinners; and purify your hearts, ye double minded*" James 4:8; Exodus 20:3.

God gives wealth – "*It is he that giveth thee power to get wealth*" Deuteronomy 8:18; "*No good thing will he withhold from them that walk uprightly*" Psalm 84:11.

Put God first – Luke 9:62; 12:29; James 1:8.

Measure success by good character, not money – "*For the Lord seeth not as man seeth; for man looketh on the outward appearance, but the Lord looketh on the heart*" 1 Samuel 16:7; "*Take heed, and beware of covetousness: for a man's life consisteth not in the abundance of the things which he possesseth*" Luke 12:15.

C. Mark "T" for True and "F" for False. *(pages 134-136)*

_____ 1. God's wisdom is not to be used to get wealth.

_____ 2. God must be the source of all, or else He is the solution to nothing.

_____ 3. Money can be a master or a servant.

_____ 4. Money is amoral.

_____ 5. Money is always bad, regardless of who has it.

_____ 6. Men have the tendency to see their worth in terms of money.

D. The proper use of money is to produce _____. *(page 136)*

1. Wherever there is righteousness, there is _____. *(page 136)*

2. Poverty is an _____. *(page 136)*

3. How would you describe a "poverty syndrome"? *(page 136)*

_____

E. It is not wrong to be rich; it is only wrong _____. *(page 139)*

For Further Study:

God is the source of all – *"For of him, and through him, and to him, are all things: to whom be glory for ever. Amen"* Romans 11:36; *"Every good gift and every perfect gift is from above, and cometh down from the Father of lights"* James 1:17.

Man gives money value – *"Charge them that are rich in this world, that they be not high-minded, nor trust in uncertain riches, but in the living God, who giveth us richly all things to enjoy"* 1 Timothy 6:17; *"For the love of money is the root of all evil: which while some coveted after, they have erred from the faith, and pierced themselves through with many sorrows"* 1 Timothy 6:10; Hebrews 12:16; 1 Peter 2:15; Jude 11.

Produce prosperity – *"And God is able to make all grace abound toward you; that ye, always having all sufficiency in all things, may abound in every good work"* 2 Corinthians 9:8.

Serve God, use money – *"Man shall not live by bread alone, but by every word that proceedeth out of the mouth of God"* Matthew 4:4; Psalm 1:1-3; Luke 12:19-21.

1. The pattern for failure is: *(page 140)*

    a. _____   c. _____

    b. _____   d. _____

2. The pattern for increase is: *(page 141)*

    a. _____   c. _____

    b. _____   d. _____

3. Make money your _____. *(page 141)*

Practical:

1. Read Proverbs 6:6-11; 12:9; 13:3; 14:4; 20:4; 20:13.

    How can you avoid poverty?

    _____

For Further Study:

Poverty is an enemy – Deuteronomy 28:47, 48; *"The thief cometh not, but for to steal, and to kill, and to destroy: I am come that they might have life, and that they might have it more abundantly"* John 10:10; Deuteronomy 8:10-17; Matthew 6:31, 32; *"And I was afraid, and went and hid thy talent in the earth: lo, there thou hast that is thine"* Matthew 25:25.

Use riches wisely – *"If riches increase, set not your heart upon them"* Psalm 62:10; 1 Timothy 6:17; *"But godliness with contentment is great gain"* 1 Timothy 6:6; Leviticus 27:30; Philippians 4:11.

2.   Rewrite 1 Timothy 6:10 **in your own words.**

_____

_____

_____

3.   Read Psalm 1:1-3 and Proverbs 13:11. What does this tell you about the WAY you earn money?

_____

4.   Memorize Deuteronomy 8:18.

Repeat this prayer out loud:

Father, in Jesus' Name, thank You for granting me a fresh start on my marriage and life. I choose today to put away uncleanness from both my marriage and my financial dealings. Help me to learn Your perspective on money, and show me where I need to repent of my old attitudes and sins. I commit to humble myself to Your ways and walk in obedience to You, so that You are glorified in my marriage and in my finances. Amen.

For Further Study:
Pattern for Increase
 Identification – Acts 2:42, 43
 Involvement – Acts 2:44
 Investment – Acts 2:45
 Increase – Acts 2:46-47
Pattern for Failure
 Deception – Genesis 3:4, 5
 Distraction – Genesis 3:6
 Dislocation – Genesis 3:7-10
 Destruction – Genesis 3:23

Self Test *Lesson 9*

1. What truly holds a marriage together? *(circle one)*

    a. romance

    b. friendship

    c. sex

2. A young man needs to know how to be a _____ to a girl, in order to be a husband to a woman.

    counselor   lover   friend

3. Sex and money are both expressions of love.   ___ True   ___ False

4. Money is the root of all evil.   ___ True   ___ False

5. What is meant by this statement: "God must be the source of all, or else He is the solution to nothing"?

    _____

    _____

6. Poverty is a Biblical sign of spirituality.   ___ True   ___ False

7. Prosperity is the natural, sequentially ordered result of _____.

8. List the pattern for failure.   9. What is the pattern for increase?

    a. _____   a. _____

    b. _____   b. _____

    c. _____   c. _____

    d. _____   d. _____

Keep this test for your own records

Lesson 10
Giving and Receiving & Debt of Love

Lesson 10
Giving and Receiving & Debt of Love

I. **Giving and Receiving (Chapter 15)**

    A. Read 1 Samuel 25. Describe a modern-day "Nabal." *(pages 144-145)*

        _____

        _____

        1. Why is tithing necessary? *(page 145)* _____

           _____

        2. God will be debtor to no man, which means man cannot _____ God. *(page 145)*

        3. What is tithing? *(page 145)* _____

           _____

        4. Name the two visible evidences of faith in God. *(page 146)*

           a. _____   b. _____

For Further Study:

Wealth is not our own doing – *"The fool hath said in his heart, There is no God"* Psalm 14:1; *"Because thou sayest, I am rich, and increased with goods, and have need of nothing; and knowest not that thou art wretched, and miserable, and poor, and blind, and naked"* Revelation 3:17; Luke 12:19-20; *"He that trusteth in his own heart is a fool: but whoso walketh wisely, he shall be delivered"* Proverbs 28:26; Psalm 107:17.

Tithing – *"Bring ye all the tithes into the storehouse ... and prove me now herewith ... if I will not open you the windows of heaven, and pour you out a blessing, that there shall not be room enough to receive it. And I will rebuke the devourer for your sakes, and he shall not destroy the fruits of your ground; neither shall your vine cast her fruit before the time in the field, saith the Lord of hosts"* Malachi 3:10-11.

We cannot out give God – *"Give, and it shall be given unto you; good measure, pressed down, and shaken together, and running over, shall men give into your bosom"* Luke 6:38.

5. How can you best tell a man's character? *(circle one) (page 146)*

    a. the use of his money   b. his way of worship

6. Moral cowardice caters to the _____ at the expense of the _____. *(page 146)*

B. Being Christ-like requires a generous spirit. *(page 147)*

    1. Describe covetousness. *(page 147)* _____

    _____

    2. Error oftentimes is nothing but _____ carried to the extreme. *(page 148)*

C. God always gives a _____ for victory. *(page 148)*

    1. Men pray for _____, and God gives a _____. *(page 148)*

    2. Name Biblical men who gained victory through a God-given strategy. *(page 148)*

        a. _____   c. _____

        b. _____   d. _____

For Further Study:

Financial health based on faith – *"He which soweth sparingly shall reap also sparingly; and he which soweth bountifully shall reap also bountifully"* 2 Corinthians 9:6; *"Honour the Lord with thy substance, and with the firstfruits of all thine increase: So shall thy barns be filled with plenty, and thy presses shall burst out with new wine"* Proverbs 3:9-10; James 2:17-20.

Jesus cares how people use money – Mark 12:41; *"Jesus said unto him, If thou wilt be perfect, go and sell that thou hast, and give to the poor, and thou shalt have treasure in heaven: and come and follow me"* Matthew 19:21; Luke 19:8; Acts 5:1-2.

Covetous v. Generous – *"It is possible to give away and become richer! It is also possible to hold on too tightly and lose everything. Yes, the liberal man shall be rich! By watering others, he waters himself"* Proverbs 11:24-25 TLB; Colossians 3:5; *"He that is greedy of gain troubleth his own house"* Proverbs 15:27; 28:27.

3. _____ is an essential component for success. *(page 149)*

4. Write out Amos 3:3.

_____

_____

D. God's promises are _____; His love is _____. *(page 149)*

E. To expect victory without being willing to fight is _____. *(page 149)*

Generosity _____ the spirit. *(page 149)*

II. **Debt of Love (Chapter 16)**

A. Read Proverbs 4:7. Wisdom is the _____ in our life. *(page 151)*

1. What is wisdom? *(page 151)* _____

2. What does wisdom provide? *(page 151)* _____

For Further Study:

Agreement – Genesis 11:6; Exodus 13:18; Amos 3:3; *"If two of you shall agree on earth as touching any thing that they shall ask, it shall be done for them of my Father which is in heaven"* Matthew 18:19.

God's love is unconditional; His promises are conditional – Hebrews 11:6; James 1:25.

Example – Promise to David – 2 Samuel 7:8; Fight to obtain it – Hebrews 11:32-33; David's strategy for victory – 2 Samuel 5:22-25

God's generosity – Psalms 84:11; 118:1; Romans 8:16-17; Ephesians 1:7

God's grace – Acts 4:33

Be Christlike – Proverbs 11:25; Romans 8:29; 2 Corinthians 3:18; Ephesians 4:32; 1 Peter 1:15-16.

Wisdom – Proverbs 4:7; *"For the Lord grants wisdom! His every word is a treasure of knowledge and understanding"* Proverbs 2:6; *"Wisdom gives: A long, good life, Riches, Honor, Pleasure, Peace"* Proverbs 3:16-17 TLB; Proverbs 8:11, 17-19, 21.

B. Name the three basic sins known to man. *(page 152)*

1. _____

2. _____

3. _____

C. Write out Romans 13:8.

_____

_____

What are some characteristics of men who are "servants of money"? *(page 153)*

1. _____

2. _____

3. _____

D. Men who are enslaved by unpaid debts are so wrapped up with _____, that they are

irresponsive to the Word of the Lord in their _____. *(page 154)*

1. Worry and debt are both _____. *(page 154)*

For Further Study:

Understanding is applied, anointed common sense – Proverbs 2:7-8; 4:5.

Jesus was tested and overcame in three areas – Matthew 4:1-9; 1 John 2:16; *"And when the devil had ended all the temptation, he departed from him for a season. And Jesus returned in the power of the Spirit into Galilee: and there went out a fame of him through all the region round about"* Luke 4:13-14; 1 John 2:15-16.

Servants of money – *"No man can serve two masters: for either he will hate the one, and love the other; or else he will hold to the one, and despise the other. Ye cannot serve God and mammon"* Matthew 6:24; *"Just as the rich rule the poor, so the borrower is servant to the lender"* Proverbs 22:7 TLB; Luke 21:34.

Get out of debt – *"Owe no man any thing, but to love one another: for he that loveth another hath fulfilled the law"* Romans 13:8; *"Be not entangled again with the yoke of bondage"* Galatians 5:1; James 4:13, 14.

2. Godliness with _____ is great gain. *(page 155)*

3. _____ is God's only method of protection for our lives. *(page 155)*

4. Financial health depends on how much you _____, not how much you _____. *(page 156)*

5. Keep adequate _____. *(page 156)*

6. How much you _____ depends on how much you _____. *(page 156)*

Practical:

1. Create a budget and get out of debt!

    a. Write out how much you owe and to whom you owe it.

    b. Covenant with your wife or prayer partner to pay off all debt.

    c. Create a monthly budget with 10% to tithes, 5% to savings, more to offerings, some to debts and the rest to living. If you can't give offerings at first, at least tithe!

For Further Study:

Be clear with debtors – *"Don't withhold repayment of your debts. Don't say 'some other time,' if you can pay now"* Proverbs 3:27-28 TLB; *"Do things in such a way that everyone can see you are honest clear through"* Romans 12:17 TLB.

Live within your means – *"Stay away from the love of money; be satisfied with what you have. For God has said, 'I will never, never fail you nor forsake you'"* Hebrews 13:5 TLB; *"Therefore take no thought, saying, What shall we eat? or, What shall we drink? or, Wherewithal shall we be clothed? ... for your heavenly Father knoweth that ye have need of all these things"* Matthew 6:31-32; *"But godliness with contentment is great gain"* 1 Timothy 6:6; *"Steady plodding brings prosperity; hasty speculation brings poverty"* Proverbs 21:5 TLB; *"Lazy people want much but get little, while the diligent are prospering"* Proverbs 13:4 TLB.

Lust is insatiable; love is easily satisfied – Ecclesiastes 5:10; 1 Corinthians 13:4; James 4:1.

Love and obedience – Deuteronomy 5:29; 1 Samuel 12:15; 2 Chronicles 16:9; Psalm 34:7; Hosea 4:6; John 14:21

2. Copy this list of ten "correct" money attitudes for your checkbook, dashboard, bathroom mirror, Bible and elsewhere so you can continually review the principles.

    The Principles of Handling Money

    1. God is your Source.

    2. Seek God first in everything.

    3. Decisions require responsibility. Decisions cannot be unilateral in marriage.

    4. Tithing is a basic visible evidence of faith.

    5. Get out of debt.

    6. Start where you are with what you have.

    7. Live within your means.

    8. To obey God today is to trust Him for tomorrow.

    9. Keep adequate records.

    10. Be generous with God — and with others.

Repeat this prayer out loud:

Father, I know I've been guilty of mismanaging my money and having wrong attitudes about it. Please forgive me. You give me the ability to earn 100% of my income. Please help me trust You with 100% of its use. I want more of my money working for Your Kingdom and less for my own desires. I repent of wrong attitudes, including a poverty mentality, and I ask You to continue to lead me into truth regarding my finances! In Jesus' Name, I pray. Amen.

For Further Study:

Financial health – Proverbs 3:17; 13:17; 21:20; 22:29

Wisdom – Strategy – Victory:

God gives wisdom for strategy – Proverbs 3:19; *"Blessed be the Lord my strength, which teacheth my hands to war, and my fingers to fight"* Psalm 144:1; *"Wisdom strengtheneth the wise more than ten mighty men which are in the city"* Ecclesiastes 7:19; Psalms 17:4; 44:5; 2 Corinthians2:14; James 1:5.

Victory requires a fight – Colossians 1:29; 1 Corinthians 9: 25-26

Victory from strategy brings glory – *"Thine, O Lord, is the greatness, and the power, and the glory, and the victory, and the majesty"* 1 Chronicles 29:11; 2 Chronicles 20:12; *"Be not afraid nor dismayed by reason of this great multitude; for the battle is not your's, but God's ... Set yourselves, stand ye still, and see the salvation of the Lord with you ... fear not, nor be dismayed ... for the Lord will be with you"* 2 Chronicles 20:15-17.

Self Test *Lesson 10*

1. Name the two visible evidences of faith in God.

    a. _____   b. _____

2. How can you best tell a man's character? *(circle one)*

    a. the use of his money   b. his way of worship

3. Generosity _____ the spirit.

4. Error oftentimes is nothing but _____ carried to the extreme.

5. Men pray for _____, and God gives a _____.

6. Name the three basic sins known to man.

    a. _____

    b. _____

    c. _____

7. What is God's means of protection? _____

8. Financial health depends on how much you _____, not how much you _____.

Keep this test for your own records

Lesson 11

The Principles of Investing

Lesson 11
The Principles of Investing

A.   Read Luke 19:12-26 — "The Law of _____ and Decline." *(page 157)*

  1.   By use you possess and gain; by _____.
       (page 158)

  2.   To gain, you must _____. *(page 158)*

  3.   Hoarding causes _____. *(page 158)*

  4.   Investing will not only allow you to keep what you have, but also _____

       _____. *(page 158)*

  5.   Where do you start investing? *(page 159)* _____

  6.   Read: *"Do not despise this small beginning, for the eyes of the Lord rejoice to see the work begin"*
       Zechariah 4:10 TLB.

B.   Name the three things men can invest. *(page 159)*

  1.   _____   2.   _____   3.   _____

C.   What do you do for twenty-four hours each day? *(page 159)* _____

For Further Study:

By use you gain; by disuse you lose – *"Because thou hast been faithful in a very little, have thou authority over ten cities"* Luke 19:17; 19:16-24; *"Unto every one which hath shall be given; and from him that hath not, even that he hath shall be taken away from him"* Luke 19:26.

Give to receive – *"Give, and it shall be given unto you; good measure, pressed down, and shaken together, and running over, shall men give into your bosom. For with the same measure that ye mete withal it shall be measured to you again"* Luke 6:38; Proverbs 11:24-25.

Start where you are with what you have – Zechariah 4:10.

D. Guidelines for investing.

1. You invest in _____. *(page 159)*

    a. A company is only as good as _____

        _____. *(page 159)*

    b. You invest in the _____ which is derived from the

        _____. *(page 160)*

    c. Read 1 Corinthians 5:11.

2. Before investing, _____. *(page 160)*

    a. Read Proverbs 14:15.

    b. Integrity is the essence of character; _____ is the cornerstone. *(page 160)*

    c. Read: *"And let the peace (soul harmony which comes) from Christ rule (act as umpire continually) in your hearts [deciding and settling with finality all questions that arise in your minds, in that peaceful state] to which as [members of Christ's] one body you were also called [to live]"* Colossians 3:15 AMP.

    d. Between these two, which is better? *(circle one) (page 161)*

        an internal witness   an external circumstance

For Further Study:

Invest in character – *"Moreover it is required in stewards, that a man be found faithful"* 1 Corinthians 4:2; *"Without wise leadership, a nation is in trouble"* Proverbs 11:14 TLB; Matthew 7:15-16; *"You are not to keep company with anyone who claims to be a brother Christian but ... is greedy, or is a swindler ... Don't even eat lunch with such a person"* 1 Corinthians 5:11 TLB; *"With good men in authority, the people rejoice; but with the wicked in power, they groan"* Proverbs 29:2 TLB; *"When there is moral rot within a nation, it's government topples easily"* Proverbs 28:2 TLB.

Investigate – *"Only a simpleton believes what he is told! A prudent man checks to see where he is going"* Proverbs 14:15 TLB; *"Any enterprise is built by wise planning, becomes strong through common sense, and profits wonderfully by keeping abreast of the facts"* Proverbs 24:3, 4 TLB.

Inner witness – *"And let the peace ... from Christ rule (act as umpire continually) in your hearts"* Colossians 3:15 AMP; *"But you have received the Holy Spirit and he lives within you, in your hearts ... he teaches you all things, and he is the Truth"* 1 John 2:27 TLB.

3. Risk, don't _____. *(page 162)*

   a. Read Proverbs 13:11.

   b. Gambling is risking on _____. *(page 162)*

   c. Knowing the _____ is vital to being able to reap the increase. *(page 162)*

   d. A wise man respects the seasons of his life and refuses to invest when _____

   _____. *(page 163)*

4. It must be put into writing. *(page 163)*   ___ True   ___ False

   a. Misunderstanding is the tool of _____. *(page 163)*

   b. If it isn't in writing, _____. *(page 163)*

   c. Never leave room for _____. *(page 164)*

5. Don't live with _____. *(page 164)*

   a. If you lose an investment, _____. *(page 164)*

   b. Jesus came to give us _____. *(page 165)*

For Further Study:

Gambling – *"Wealth from gambling quickly disappears; wealth from hard work grows"* Proverbs 13:11 TLB.
Learn the seasons – *"To every thing there is a season, and a time for every purpose under the heaven"*
Ecclesiastes 3:1; *"Preach the word; be instant in season and out of season"* 2 Timothy 4:2.
Impatience and misunderstanding – Hebrews 10:36; *"Reliable communication permits progress"* Proverbs 13:17 TLB.
Put it in writing – *"In everyday life a promise made by one man to another, if it is written down and signed, cannot be changed"* Galatians 3:15 TLB; Nehemiah 9:38; *"He who became the great Shepherd of the sheep by an everlasting agreement between God and you, signed with his blood"* Hebrews 13:20 TLB; *"And he wrote upon the tables the words of the covenant, the ten commandments"* Exodus 34:28.
Bury failures – *"But this one thing I do, forgetting those things which are behind, and reaching forth unto those things which are before"* Philippians 3:13; 1 Samuel 16:1; Proverbs 28:13; John 10:10; Romans 7:24-8:1.

6. Invest in talkers. *(page 165)* ___ True ___ False

    a. The man who _____ the least _____ the most. *(page 165)*

    b. Name three attributes of men with whom you should invest. *(page 166)*

    _____   _____   _____

7. _____ are more fierce than reality. *(page 166)*

    a. Shadows are what we think others _____. *(page 166)*

    b. What casts the biggest shadow? *(page 168)* _____

8. Where do funds come from? *(page 168)* _____

    a. Repeat business comes from those who _____. *(page 168)*

    b. An investment to make a friend will pay _____ than any company. *(page 168)*

    c. Read Luke 16:9.

9. Invest your _____ for your greatest good. *(page 169)*

For Further Study:

Talkers v. Producers – Proverbs 12:11; 13:4; Luke 19:20-22; *"Iron sharpeneth iron; so a man sharpeneth the countenance of his friend"* Proverbs 27:17; *"Work brings profit; talk brings poverty!"* Proverbs 14:23 TLB.

Fear – *"For God hath not given us the spirit of fear; but of power, and of love, and of a sound mind"* 2 Timothy 1:7; *"The wicked flee when no man pursueth; but the righteous are bold as a lion"* Proverbs 28:1; Genesis 3:10; Psalm 119:105. *"There is no fear in love; but perfect love casteth out fear: because fear has torment"* 1 John 4:18.

Guilt is a killer – Psalm 32:3-5; Matthew 6:12; Romans 12:2.

Friends – *"Never abandon a friend – either yours or your father's"* Proverbs 27:10 TLB; *"And I tell you, make friend for yourselves by means of unrighteous mammon [that is, deceitful riches, money, possessions], so that when it fails, they [those you have favored] may receive and welcome you into the everlasting habitations (dwellings)"* Luke 16:9 AMP.

    a.   Any investment is always an investment _____. *(page 169)*

    b.   Where you invest your money reveals _____.
        (page 169)

    c.   Your life is your _____. *(page 170)*

10. Never, never, never, never _____! *(page 170)*

Practical:

1.   Read: *"Your own friend and your father's friend, forsake them not; neither go to your brother's house in the day of your calamity. Better is a neighbor who is near [in spirit] than a brother who is far off [in heart]"* Proverbs 27:10 AMP.

     How can you make friends whom you'll be able to count on some day for help?

     _____

     _____

For Further Study:

Invest in yourself – *"For where your treasure is, there will your heart be also"* Matthew 6:21.

Your life is in your giving – Proverbs 11:24-25; Luke 21:1-5; Matthew 6:33; 10:39; 20:28.

Don't quit – *"And let us not be weary in well doing: for in due season we shall reap, if we faint not"* Galatians 6:9.

3. Is investing to ensure you make money a bad motivation? What about if other people don't make as much as you?

    _____

    _____

Repeat this prayer out loud:

Father, in Jesus' Name, I thank You for the revelation that investing is really planting my own life. Thank You for granting me the wisdom to be wise in my investing. Help me to become purified of all wrong desires for money. But help me to make money that will further Your Kingdom on this earth. Help me be a giver, not a taker, Lord. I invest my one life wholly in You. Amen.

Principles I want to memorize:

Self Test *Lesson 11*

1. What you don't use, you _____.

2. Men can invest three things.

   a. _____   b. _____   c. _____

3. As long as a company is doing well financially, it doesn't matter what the character of the corporate

   officers are.   ___ True   ___ False

4. _____ is the essence of character.

5. _____ is the umpire for doing the will of God.

6. An _____ is always better than an external circumstance.

7. Risk is different than gambling. Gambling is risking on _____.

8. If it isn't in writing, it _____.

9. If you lose an investment: *(circle one)*

   a. investigate it   b. bury it   c. learn to live with it

10. The man who does the least, _____.

11. Guilt is a _____.

12. The wisest investment is in: *(circle one)*

    a. companies   b. friends

13. God never, never, never wants me to: *(circle one)*

    a. cry   b. fail   c. quit

Keep this test for your own records

Lesson 12

But the Greatest of These Is Love & Do It!

Lesson 12
But the Greatest of These Is Love & Do It!

I.   **But the Greatest of These Is Love (Chapter 18)**

    A.   Name the three most powerful words in the human vocabulary. *(page 173)* _____

        1.   The strongest thing known to man is: *(circle one)* *(page 173)*

            a. an ox   b. superglue   c. love

        2.   God describes Himself as _____. *(page 174)*

    B.   What is the difference between knowing the joy of Heaven or the grief of Hell? *(page 174)*

        _____

        1.   _____ is the only kind of love God knows. *(page 175)*

        2.   Write out Revelation 2:4. _____

        _____

    C.   When we sin, we don't lose our salvation, only _____. *(page 175)*

        1.   Read Psalm 51:12.

        2.   After sinning with Bathsheba, David knew his salvation was still there, but the _____ had gone. *(page 175)*

        3.   The way it returns is through _____, which leads to restoration. *(page 175)*

For Further Study:

God's love – *"And hope maketh not ashamed; because the love of God is shed abroad in our hearts by the Holy Ghost which is given unto us"* Romans 5:5; 2 Corinthians 5:17; 1 John 4:7-8; 9-12; Romans 8:35-37; John 17:20-21; John 17:23 TLB. First love – John 4:14; 7:38; Revelation 2:4-5

D.   God could never be described as having "tough love." *(page 175)* ___ True ___ False

   1.   We don't have to convince God to give us anything. *(page 176)* ___ True ___ False

   2.   Write out Psalm 84:11.

   _____

   _____

   3.   God's _____ are an evidence of His tough love. *(page 176)*

   4.   "Others may, _____" is what God tells those who desire His greatness and excellence in their lives. *(page 177)*

   5.   Describe mediocre men. *(circle one) (page 177)*

   _____

E.   God's conviction of sin in our lives is for our: *(circle one) (page 177)*

   education   good   guilt

   What is God's motive for convicting us of sin? *(page 177)*

   _____

For Further Study:

God's love – *"But God commendeth his love toward us, in that, while we were yet sinners, Christ died for us … For if, when we were enemies, we were reconciled to God by the death of his Son, much more, being reconciled, we shall be saved by his life"* Romans 5:8, 10; *"Fear not, little flock; for it is your Father's good pleasure to give you the kingdom"* Luke 12:32; *"He that spared not his own Son, but delivered him up for us all, how shall he not with him also freely give us all things?"* Romans 8:32; Philippians 4:19; 2 Peter 1:3.
Truth in love – *"But speaking the truth in love"* Ephesians 4:15; Deuteronomy 5:29
Satan's lie – God keeps you from having a good time – Genesis 3:4-5; *"He keepeth the paths of judgment, and preserveth the way of his saints"* Proverbs 2:8.
Obedience – *"Cursed be the man that obeyeth not the words of this covenant"* Jeremiah 11:3; *"And a curse, if ye will not obey the commandments of the Lord your God"* Deuteronomy 11:28.
Others may, you cannot – 2 Timothy 2:19-21.

F.   Love centers in _____. *(page 178)*

G.   Name the three evidences of love. *(page 178)*

1.   _____

2.   _____

3.   _____

H.   God never stops working for my _____. *(page 178)*

1.   Nothing impersonal can ever truly _____. *(page 179)*

2.   Why does God love us? *(page 179)* _____

3.   Real men should never say, "I love you," because it's a sign of weakness. *(page 179)*

___ True   ___ False

II.   **Do It! (Chapter 19)**

A.   In marriage, a sense of "oneness" is vitally important. *(page 181)*   ___ True   ___ False

1.   In a troubled marriage, both men and women use a weapon to try to gain power over the other.

(page 183)   ___ True   ___ False

For Further Study:

Mediocrity – 2 Chronicles 25:2; *"My people mingle with the heathen, picking up their evil ways; thus they become as good-for-nothing as a half-baked cake!"* Hosea 7:8 TLB. God challenges us – *"As many as I love, I rebuke and chasten; be zealous therefore, and repent"* Revelations 3:19; Hebrews 12:5-8; 1 Peter 1:6-7; 1 Corinthians 11:32.
Repentance – Psalm 34:14-16; 2 Corinthians 16:17; James 1:27; 1 John 1:9
Receiving – Matthew 10:8; *"What things soever ye desire, when ye pray, believe that ye receive them, and ye shall have them"* Mark 11:24; James 1:21. God is always working for our highest good – Romans 8:28.
Evidences – Selflessness – 1 Corinthians 13:4-5; Desire for unity – John 17:20-21; Desire to benefit the one loved – 1 Corinthians 13:7 TLB.
Love requires relationship – John 14:23; not impersonal – John 4:13-14.

2. Men often use the power of _____. *(page 183)*

3. Women often use the power of _____. *(page 183)*

B. Praying together produces _____. *(page 186)*

1. Praying together and continually telling each other "I love you" are vitally important. *(page 186)*

___ True ___ False

2. Some men wait too late to _____. *(page 186)*

C. What day is today for you? *(page 186)* _____

_____

Practical:
1. When is the last time you took your wife away alone? Plan now, book now, schedule now.
2. Get out a calendar and plan one day/night each week for your children. Pray and let God guide you to activities that will cause lasting memories in your children and family.

Repeat this prayer out loud:

Father, in Jesus' Name, I realize that You loved me first, while I was yet dead in my sins and trespasses. I want to love even when others are in sin, like You did with me. Help me to be a living example of Your love and grace to my wife and family. Please teach me how to be a skillful communicator of Your character to them. Amen.

For Further Study:
God is personal – Jeremiah 31:3; 1 John 4:16; John 14:6; *"For as you know him better, he will give you, through his great power, everything you need for living a truly good life"* 2 Peter 1:3 TLB.
Say and live "I love you" – Proverbs 27:5; Ephesians 5:28; *"Love never faileth"* 1 Corinthians 13:8.
Oneness – Mark 10:7-8; James 3:16
Make changes – Jeremiah 8:20; Ephesians 4:26 TLB; *"Today if you will hear his voice, Harden not your hearts"* Hebrews 3:7-8.

Self Test *Lesson 12*

1. What are the most powerful words in the human vocabulary? _____

2. After sinning with Bathsheba, David cried out:

    _____

3. David was aware, after sinning with Bathsheba, that he had lost his salvation.   ___ True ___ False

4. God's love is _____, but His promises are _____.

5. White lines down the middle of the highway are evidence that people in the highway department hate you.

    ___ True   ___ False

    Why are those lines there? _____

    Why are God's commandments "there"? _____

6. Mediocre men settle for _____, which is the enemy of _____.

7. Name love's three evidences.

    a. _____

    b. _____

    c. _____

8. What do men and women turn into weapons in a troubled marriage?

    a. Men: _____   b. Women: _____

9. When is the best time to change? *(circle one)*

    a. tomorrow   b. later   c. now

Keep this test for your own records

Final Exam

1. Fame can come in a moment, but greatness _____ .

2. God created man in His image for His glory and created the woman: *(circle one)*
   a. for the enjoyment of the man
   b. for the glory of the man
   c. to take care of the man

3. Mediocre men want authority without: *(circle one)*

   a. marriage   b. position   c. accountability

4. Becoming a Christ-like man is a quick and easy process.   ___ True ___ False

5. Christianity teaches that women should be subjugated and put down.

   ___ True ___ False

6. All good communication in life must begin with what? _____

7. Which is more important – the day before the battle or the day after the battle? _____

8. The closer a lie is to the truth, the more damning it is.   ___ True ___ False

9. A man's name is only as good as his _____ .

10. God never gives authority without: *(circle one)*

    a. mercy   b. salvation   c. accountability

11. Circle the three main evidences of a changed life in conversion.
    a. a love for God
    b. a desire for hours of prayer
    c. a burden for world missions
    d. a love for the Word
    e. a love of the brethren

12. To small children, what is the difference between a broken promise and a lie from their father? _____

13. What acts as an "umpire" for doing the will of God? _____

DETACH HERE

14. What are great works built on? _____

15. A woman should be able to trust a man, even when he doesn't keep his word.

    ___ True   ___ False

16. Love desires to _____ others at the _____.

17. Great men are known by the greatness of their _____.

18. Stability in a man's character translates to _____ in his children.

19. Every word we speak releases the _____ in which it is spoken.

20. If you want to change your emotions, change your _____.

21. Sex is an external evidence of an _____ and _____

    _____.

22. Lust desires to gratify self at the expense of _____.

23. Love desires to benefit others even at the expense of _____.

24. Any sex outside of marriage is _____.

25. Sons who do not forgive the sins of their fathers often make the same mistakes with their sons.

    ___ True   ___ False

26. Sin promises to _____ and _____, but only desires to _____ and _____.

27. When a man forces his wife to do something contrary to her consecration and coerces her to do something

    outside of faith, it is wrong.   ___ True   ___ False

28. Where does change begin? _____

29. What is one of the most important ways a man ministers to his wife? _____

DETACH HERE

30. To God, and the godly, virginity is a _____.

31. God does not demand that a man be a virgin when he marries.   ___ True ___ False

32. It is not possible to prove the virginity of a man. The man's _____ was to be reliable.

33. When a husband and wife have their first time of sexual intimacy, it is a sign before God that they have

entered into a _____.

34. You cannot receive your virginity again physically, but you can receive it again spiritually.

___ True   ___ False

35. A young man needs to know how to be a _____ to a girl in order to be a husband to a woman.

counselor   lover   friend

36. Sex and money are both expressions of love.   ___ True ___ False

37. Money is the root of all evil.   ___ True ___ False

38. List the pattern for failure.

a. _____   c. _____

b. _____   d. _____

39. What is the pattern for increase?

a. _____   c. _____

b. _____   d. _____

40. Name the two visible evidences of faith in God.

a. _____

b. _____

DETACH HERE

Final Exam

41. Generosity _____ the spirit.

42. Error oftentimes is nothing but _____ carried to the extreme.

43. Name the three basic sins known to man.

   a. _____ b. _____ c. _____

44. If it isn't in writing, it _____.

45. If you lose an investment: *(circle one)*

   a. investigate it   b. bury it   c. learn to live with it

46. The wisest investment is in: *(circle one)*   a. companies   b. friends

47. God never, never, never wants me to: *(circle one)*   a. cry   b. fail   c. quit

48. What are the most powerful words in the human vocabulary? _____

49. God's love is _____, but His promises are _____.

50. White lines down the middle of the highway are evidence that people in the highway department hate you.

   ___ True   ___ False

   Why are those lines there? _____

   Why are God's commandments "there"? _____

51. Mediocre men settle for _____, which is the enemy of _____.

52. Name love's three evidences.

   a. _____

   b. _____

   c. _____

Final Exam

53. What do men and women turn into weapons in a troubled marriage?

    a. Men: _____   b. Women: _____

54. When is the best time to change? *(circle one)*   a. tomorrow   b. later   c. now

55. Short Essay — *"If you don't communicate, you can't relate."* All relationships are based on good communications. Words have power. A man's word is his bond. Summarize what impact these truths make on all your relationships — now and in the future.

    _____

    _____

    _____

    _____

    _____

    _____

    _____

    _____

Name _____

Address _____ City _____ State____ Zip_____

Telephone   a.m. _____   p.m. _____

Email Address _____

The Final Exam is required to be "commissioned."

For more information, contact
Christian Men's Network | P.O. Box 3 | Grapevine, TX 76099
ChristianMensNetwork.com | office@ChristianMensNetwork.com | 817-437-4888

DETACH HERE

Basic Daily Bible Reading

Read Proverbs each morning for wisdom, Psalms each evening for courage. Make copies of this chart and keep it in your Bible to mark off as you read. If you are just starting the habit of Bible reading, be aware that longer translations or paraphrases (such as Amplified and Living) will take longer to read each day. As you start, it is okay to read only one of the chapters in Psalms each night, instead of the many listed. Mark your chart so you'll remember which ones you haven't read.
NOTE: The chronological chart following has the rest of the chapters of Psalms that are not listed here. By using both charts together, you will cover the entire book of Psalms.

Day of Month	Proverbs	Psalms	Day of Month	Proverbs	Psalms
1	1	1, 2, 4, 5, 6	18	18	82, 83, 84, 85
2	2	7, 8, 9	19	19	87, 88, 91, 92
3	3	10, 11, 12, 13, 14, 15	20	20	93, 94, 95, 97
4	4	16, 17, 19, 20	21	21	98, 99, 100, 101, 103
5	5	21, 22, 23	22	22	104, 108
6	6	24, 25, 26, 27	23	23	109, 110, 111
7	7	28, 29, 31, 32	24	24	112, 113, 114, 115, 117
8	8	33, 35	25	25	119:1-56
9	9	36, 37	26	26	119:57-112
10	10	38, 39, 40	27	27	119:113-176
11	11	41, 42, 43, 45, 46	28	28	120, 121, 122, 124, 130, 131, 133, 134
12	12	47, 48, 49, 50			
13	13	53, 55, 58, 61, 62	29	29	135, 136, 138
14	14	64, 65, 66, 67	30	30	139, 140, 141, 143
15	15	68, 69	31	31	144, 145, 146, 148, 150
16	16	70, 71, 73			
17	17	75, 76, 77, 81			

Chronological Annual Bible Reading

This schedule follows the events of the Bible chronologically and can be used with any translation or paraphrase of the Bible. Each day has an average of 77 verses of Scripture. If you follow this annually, along with your Daily Bible Reading, by your third year, you will recognize where you are and what is going to happen next. By your fifth year, you will understand the Scriptural background and setting for any reference spoken of in a message or book. At that point, the Word will become more like "meat" to you and less like "milk." Once you understand the basic stories and what happens on the surface, God can reveal to you the layers of meaning beneath. So, make copies of this chart to keep in your Bible and mark off as you read. And start reading—it's the greatest adventure in life!

Some notes:
1. Some modern translations don't have verses numbered (such as The Message), so they cannot be used with this chart. Also, if you are just starting the Bible, be aware that longer translations or paraphrases (such as Amplified and Living) tend to take longer to read each day.
2. The Daily Bible Reading chart covers the Proverbs and the chapters of Psalms that are not listed here. By using both charts together, you will cover the entire books of Psalms and Proverbs along with the rest of the Bible.
3. The chronology of Scripture is obvious in some cases, educated guesswork in others. The placement of Job, for example, is purely conjecture since there is no consensus among Bible scholars as to its date or place. For the most part, however, chronological reading helps the reader, since it places stories that have duplicated information, or prophetic utterances elsewhere in Scripture, within the same reading sequence.

HOW TO READ SCRIPTURE NOTATIONS:
Book chapter: verse. (Mark 15:44 means the book of Mark, chapter 15, verse 44.)
Book chapter; chapter (Mark 15; 16; 17 means the book of Mark, chapters 15, 16, 17.)
Books continue the same until otherwise noted. (2 Kings 22; 23:1-28; Jeremiah 20 means the book of 2 Kings, chapter 22, the book of 2 Kings, chapter 23, verses 1-28; then the book of Jeremiah, chapter 20.)

1	Jan 1	Genesis 1; 2; 3
2	Jan 2	Genesis 4; 5; 6
3	Jan 3	Genesis 7; 8; 9
4	Jan 4	Genesis 10; 11; 12
5	Jan 5	Genesis 13; 14; 15; 16
6	Jan 6	Genesis 17; 18; 19:1-29
7	Jan 7	Genesis 19:30-38; 20; 21
8	Jan 8	Genesis 22; 23; 24:1-31
9	Jan 9	Genesis 24:32-67; 25
10	Jan 10	Genesis 26; 27
11	Jan 11	Genesis 28; 29; 30:1-24
12	Jan 12	Genesis 30:25-43; 31
13	Jan 13	Genesis 32; 33; 34
14	Jan 14	Genesis 35; 36
15	Jan 15	Genesis 37; 38; 39
16	Jan 16	Genesis 40; 41
17	Jan 17	Genesis 42; 43
18	Jan 18	Genesis 44; 45
19	Jan 19	Genesis 46; 47; 48
20	Jan 20	Genesis 49; 50; Exodus 1
21	Jan 21	Exodus 2; 3; 4
22	Jan 22	Exodus 5; 6; 7
23	Jan 23	Exodus 8; 9
24	Jan 24	Exodus 10; 11; 12
25	Jan 25	Exodus 13; 14; 15
26	Jan 26	Exodus 16; 17; 18
27	Jan 27	Exodus 19; 20; 21
28	Jan 28	Exodus 22; 23; 24
29	Jan 29	Exodus 25; 26
30	Jan 30	Exodus 27; 28; 29:1-28
31	Jan 31	Exodus 29:29-46; 30; 31
32	Feb 1	Exodus 32; 33; 34
33	Feb 2	Exodus 35; 36
34	Feb 3	Exodus 37; 38
35	Feb 4	Exodus 39; 40
36	Feb 5	Leviticus 1; 2; 3; 4
37	Feb 6	Leviticus 5; 6; 7
38	Feb 7	Leviticus 8; 9; 10
39	Feb 8	Leviticus 11; 12; 13:1-37
40	Feb 9	Leviticus 13:38-59; 14
41	Feb 10	Leviticus 15; 16
42	Feb 11	Leviticus 17; 18; 19
43	Feb 12	Leviticus 20; 21; 22:1-16
44	Feb 13	Leviticus 22:17-33; 23
45	Feb 14	Leviticus 24; 25
46	Feb 15	Leviticus 26; 27
47	Feb 16	Numbers 1; 2
48	Feb 17	Numbers 3; 4:1-20
49	Feb 18	Numbers 4:21-49; 5; 6
50	Feb 19	Numbers 7
51	Feb 20	Numbers 8; 9; 10
52	Feb 21	Numbers 11; 12; 13
53	Feb 22	Numbers 14; 15
54	Feb 23	Numbers 16; 17
55	Feb 24	Numbers 18; 19; 20
56	Feb 25	Numbers 21; 22
57	Feb 26	Numbers 23; 24; 25
58	Feb 27	Numbers 26; 27
59	Feb 28	Numbers 28; 29; 30
60	Mar 1	Numbers 31; 32:1-27
61	Mar 2	Numbers 32:28-42; 33
62	Mar 3	Numbers 34; 35; 36
63	Mar 4	Deuteronomy 1; 2
64	Mar 5	Deuteronomy 3; 4
65	Mar 6	Deuteronomy 5; 6; 7
66	Mar 7	Deuteronomy 8; 9; 10
67	Mar 8	Deuteronomy 11; 12; 13
68	Mar 9	Deuteronomy 14; 15; 16
69	Mar 10	Deuteronomy 17; 18; 19; 20
70	Mar 11	Deuteronomy 21; 22; 23
71	Mar 12	Deuteronomy 24; 25; 26; 27
72	Mar 13	Deuteronomy 28
73	Mar 14	Deuteronomy 29; 30; 31
74	Mar 15	Deuteronomy 32; 33
75	Mar 16	Deuteronomy 34; Psalm 90; Joshua 1; 2
76	Mar 17	Joshua 3; 4; 5; 6
77	Mar 18	Joshua 7; 8; 9
78	Mar 19	Joshua 10; 11
79	Mar 20	Joshua 12; 13; 14
80	Mar 21	Joshua 15; 16
81	Mar 22	Joshua 17; 18; 19:1-23
82	Mar 23	Joshua 19:24-51; 20; 21
83	Mar 24	Joshua 22; 23; 24
84	Mar 25	Judges 1; 2; 3:1-11
85	Mar 26	Judges 3:12-31; 4; 5
86	Mar 27	Judges 6; 7
87	Mar 28	Judges 8; 9
88	Mar 29	Judges 10; 11; 12
89	Mar 30	Judges 13; 14; 15
90	Mar 31	Judges 16; 17; 18
91	Apr 1	Judges 19; 20

[You have completed 1/4 of the Bible!]

92	Apr 2	Judges 21; Job 1; 2; 3
93	Apr 3	Job 4; 5; 6
94	Apr 4	Job 7; 8; 9
95	Apr 5	Job 10; 11; 12
96	Apr 6	Job 13; 14; 15
97	Apr 7	Job 16; 17; 18; 19
98	Apr 8	Job 20; 21
99	Apr 9	Job 22; 23; 24
100	Apr 10	Job 25; 26; 27; 28
101	Apr 11	Job 29; 30; 31
102	Apr 12	Job 32; 33; 34
103	Apr 13	Job 35; 36; 37
104	Apr 14	Job 38; 39
105	Apr 15	Job 40; 41; 42
106	Apr 16	Ruth 1; 2; 3
107	Apr 17	Ruth 4; 1 Samuel 1; 2
108	Apr 18	1 Samuel 3; 4; 5; 6
109	Apr 19	1 Samuel 7; 8; 9
110	Apr 20	1 Samuel 10; 11; 12; 13
111	Apr 21	1 Samuel 14; 15
112	Apr 22	1 Samuel 16; 17
113	Apr 23	1 Samuel 18; 19; Psalm 59
114	Apr 24	1 Samuel 20; 21; Psalms 34; 56
115	Apr 25	1 Samuel 22; 23, Psalms 52; 142
116	Apr 26	1 Samuel 24; 25; 1 Chronicles 12:8-18; Psalm 57
117	Apr 27	1 Samuel 26; 27; 28; Psalms 54; 63
118	Apr 28	1 Samuel 29; 30; 31; 1 Chronicles 12:1-7; 12:19-22
119	Apr 29	1 Chronicles 10; 2 Samuel 1; 2
120	Apr 30	2 Samuel 3; 4; 1 Chronicles 11:1-9; 12:23-40
121	May 1	2 Samuel 5; 6; 1 Chronicles 13; 14
122	May 2	2 Samuel 22; 1 Chronicles 15
123	May 3	1 Chronicles 16; Psalm 18
124	May 4	2 Samuel 7; Psalms 96; 105
125	May 5	1 Chronicles 17; 2 Samuel 8; 9; 10
126	May 6	1 Chronicles 18; 19; Psalm 60; 2 Samuel 11
127	May 7	2 Samuel 12; 13; 1 Chronicles 20:1-3; Psalm 51
128	May 8	2 Samuel 14; 15
129	May 9	2 Samuel 16; 17; 18; Psalm 3
130	May 10	2 Samuel 19; 20; 21
131	May 11	2 Samuel 23:8-23
132	May 12	1 Chronicles 20:4-8; 11:10-25; 2 Samuel 23:24-39; 24
133	May 13	1 Chronicles 11:26-47; 21; 22
134	May 14	1 Chronicles 23; 24; Psalm 30
135	May 15	1 Chronicles 25; 26
136	May 16	1 Chronicles 27; 28; 29
137	May 17	1 Kings 1; 2:1-12; 2 Samuel 23:1-7
138	May 18	1 Kings 2:13-46; 3; 2 Chronicles 1:1-13
139	May 19	1 Kings 5; 6; 2 Chronicles 2
140	May 20	1 Kings 7; 2 Chronicles 3; 4
141	May 21	1 Kings 8; 2 Chronicles 5
142	May 22	1 Kings 9; 2 Chronicles 6; 7:1-10
143	May 23	1 Kings 10:1-13; 2 Chronicles 7:11-22; 8; 9:1-12; 1 Kings 4
144	May 24	1 Kings 10:14-29; 2 Chronicles 1:14-17; 9:13-28; Psalms 72; 127
145	May 25	Song of Solomon 1; 2; 3; 4; 5
146	May 26	Song of Solomon 6; 7; 8; 1 Kings 11:1-40
147	May 27	Ecclesiastes 1; 2; 3; 4
148	May 28	Ecclesiastes 5; 6; 7; 8
149	May 29	Ecclesiastes 9; 10; 11; 12; 1 Kings 11:41-43; 2 Chronicles 9:29-31
150	May 30	1 Kings 12; 2 Chronicles 10; 11
151	May 31	1 Kings 13; 14; 2 Chronicles 12
152	June 1	1 Kings 15; 2 Chronicles 13; 14; 15
153	June 2	1 Kings 16; 2 Chronicles 16; 17
154	June 3	1 Kings 17; 18; 19
155	June 4	1 Kings 20; 21
156	June 5	1 Kings 22; 2 Chronicles 18
157	June 6	2 Kings 1; 2; 2 Chronicles 19; 20; 21:1-3
158	June 7	2 Kings 3; 4
159	June 8	2 Kings 5; 6; 7
160	June 9	2 Kings 8; 9; 2 Chronicles 21:4-20
161	June 10	2 Chronicles 22; 23; 2 Kings 10; 11
162	June 11	Joel 1; 2; 3
163	June 12	2 Kings 12; 13; 2 Chronicles 24
164	June 13	2 Kings 14; 2 Chronicles 25; Jonah 1
165	June 14	Jonah 2; 3; 4; Hosea 1; 2; 3; 4
166	June 15	Hosea 5; 6; 7; 8; 9; 10
167	June 16	Hosea 11; 12; 13; 14
168	June 17	2 Kings 15:1-7; 2 Chronicles 26; Amos 1; 2; 3
169	June 18	Amos 4; 5; 6; 7
170	June 19	Amos 8; 9; 2 Kings 15:8-18; Isaiah 1

DETACH HERE

171	June 20	Isaiah 2; 3; 4; 2 Kings 15:19-38; 2 Chronicles 27
172	June 21	Isaiah 5; 6; Micah 1; 2; 3
173	June 22	Micah 4; 5; 6; 7; 2 Kings 16:1-18
174	June 23	2 Chronicles 28; Isaiah 7; 8
175	June 24	Isaiah 9; 10; 11; 12
176	June 25	Isaiah 13; 14; 15; 16
177	June 26	Isaiah 17; 18; 19; 20; 21
178	June 27	Isaiah 22; 23; 24; 25
179	June 28	Isaiah 26; 27; 28; 29
180	June 29	Isaiah 30; 31; 32; 33
181	June 30	Isaiah 34; 35; 2 Kings 18:1-8; 2 Chronicles 29
182	July 1	2 Chronicles 30; 31; 2 Kings 17; 2 Kings 16:19-20

[You have completed 1/2 of the Bible!]

183	July 2	2 Kings 18:9-37; 2 Chronicles 32:1-19; Isaiah 36
184	July 3	2 Kings 19; 2 Chronicles 32:20-23; Isaiah 37
185	July 4	2 Kings 20; 21:1-18; 2 Chronicles 32:24-33; Isaiah 38; 39
186	July 5	2 Chronicles 33:1-20; Isaiah 40; 41
187	July 6	Isaiah 42; 43; 44
188	July 7	Isaiah 45; 46; 47; 48
189	July 8	Isaiah 49; 50; 51; 52
190	July 9	Isaiah 53; 54; 55; 56; 57
191	July 10	Isaiah 58; 59; 60; 61; 62
192	July 11	Isaiah 63; 64; 65; 66
193	July 12	2 Kings 21:19-26; 2 Chronicles 33:21-25; 34:1-7; Zephaniah 1; 2; 3
194	July 13	Jeremiah 1; 2; 3
195	July 14	Jeremiah 4; 5
196	July 15	Jeremiah 6; 7; 8
197	July 16	Jeremiah 9; 10; 11
198	July 17	Jeremiah 12; 13; 14; 15
199	July 18	Jeremiah 16; 17; 18; 19
200	July 19	Jeremiah 20; 2 Kings 22; 23:1-28
201	July 20	2 Chronicles 34:8-33; 35:1-19; Nahum 1; 2; 3
202	July 21	2 Kings 23:29-37; 2 Chronicles 35:20-27; 36:1-5; Jeremiah 22:10-17; 26; Habakkuk 1
203	July 22	Habakkuk 2; 3; Jeremiah 46; 47; 2 Kings 24:1-4; 2 Chronicles 36:6-7
204	July 23	Jeremiah 25; 35; 36; 45
205	July 24	Jeremiah 48; 49:1-33
206	July 25	Daniel 1; 2
207	July 26	Jeremiah 22:18-30; 2 Kings 24:5-20; 2 Chronicles 36:8-12; Jeremiah 37:1-2; 52:1-3; 24; 29
208	July 27	Jeremiah 27; 28; 23
209	July 28	Jeremiah 50; 51:1-19
210	July 29	Jeremiah 51:20-64; 49:34-39; 34
211	July 30	Ezekiel 1; 2; 3; 4
212	July 31	Ezekiel 5; 6; 7; 8
213	Aug 1	Ezekiel 9; 10; 11; 12
214	Aug 2	Ezekiel 13, 14, 15, 16:1-34
215	Aug 3	Ezekiel 16:35-63; 17; 18
216	Aug 4	Ezekiel 19; 20
217	Aug 5	Ezekiel 21; 22

218	Aug 6	Ezekiel 23; 2 Kings 25:1; 2 Chronicles 36:13-16; Jeremiah 39:1; 52:4; Ezekiel 24
219	Aug 7	Jeremiah 21; 22:1-9; 32; 30
220	Aug 8	Jeremiah 31; 33; Ezekiel 25
221	Aug 9	Ezekiel 29:1-16; 30; 31; 26
222	Aug 10	Ezekiel 27; 28; Jeremiah 37:3-21
223	Aug 11	Jeremiah 38; 39:2-10; 52:5-30
224	Aug 12	2 Kings 25:2-22; 2 Chronicles 36:17-21; Jeremiah 39:11-18; 40:1-6; Lamentations 1
225	Aug 13	Lamentations 2; 3
226	Aug 14	Lamentations 4; 5; Obadiah; Jeremiah 40:7-16
227	Aug 15	Jeremiah 41; 42; 43; 44; 2 Kings 25:23-26
228	Aug 16	Ezekiel 33:21-33; 34; 35; 36
229	Aug 17	Ezekiel 37; 38; 39
230	Aug 18	Ezekiel 32; 33:1-20; Daniel 3
231	Aug 19	Ezekiel 40; 41
232	Aug 20	Ezekiel 42; 43; 44
233	Aug 21	Ezekiel 45; 46; 47
234	Aug 22	Ezekiel 48; 29:17-21; Daniel 4
235	Aug 23	Jeremiah 52:31-34; 2 Kings 25:27-30; Psalms 44; 74; 79
236	Aug 24	Psalms 80; 86; 89
237	Aug 25	Psalms 102; 106
238	Aug 26	Psalms 123; 137; Daniel 7; 8
239	Aug 27	Daniel 5; 9; 6
240	Aug 28	2 Chronicles 36:22-23; Ezra 1; 2
241	Aug 29	Ezra 3; 4:1-5; Daniel 10; 11
242	Aug 30	Daniel 12; Ezra 4:6-24; 5; 6:1-13; Haggai 1
243	Aug 31	Haggai 2; Zechariah 1; 2; 3
244	Sept 1	Zechariah 4; 5; 6; 7; 8
245	Sept 2	Ezra 6:14-22; Psalm 78
246	Sept 3	Psalms 107; 116; 118
247	Sept 4	Psalms 125; 126; 128; 129; 132; 147
248	Sept 5	Psalm 149; Zechariah 9; 10; 11; 12; 13
249	Sept 6	Zechariah 14; Esther 1; 2; 3
250	Sept 7	Esther 4; 5; 6; 7; 8
251	Sept 8	Esther 9; 10; Ezra 7; 8
252	Sept 9	Ezra 9; 10; Nehemiah 1
253	Sept 10	Nehemiah 2; 3; 4; 5
254	Sept 11	Nehemiah 6; 7
255	Sept 12	Nehemiah 8; 9; 10
256	Sept 13	Nehemiah 11; 12
257	Sept 14	Nehemiah 13; Malachi 1; 2; 3; 4
258	Sept 15	1 Chronicles 1; 2:1-35
259	Sept 16	1 Chronicles 2:36-55; 3; 4
260	Sept 17	1 Chronicles 5; 6:1-41
261	Sept 18	1 Chronicles 6:42-81; 7
262	Sept 19	1 Chronicles 8; 9
263	Sept 20	Matthew 1; 2; 3; 4
264	Sept 21	Matthew 5; 6
265	Sept 22	Matthew 7; 8
266	Sept 23	Matthew 9; 10
267	Sept 24	Matthew 11; 12
268	Sept 25	Matthew 13; 14
269	Sept 26	Matthew 15; 16
270	Sept 27	Matthew 17; 18; 19

271	Sept 28	Matthew 20; 21
272	Sept 29	Matthew 22; 23
273	Sept 30	Matthew 24; 25

[You have completed 3/4 of the Bible!]

274	Oct 1	Matthew 26; 27; 28
275	Oct 2	Mark 1; 2
276	Oct 3	Mark 3; 4
277	Oct 4	Mark 5; 6
278	Oct 5	Mark 7; 8:1-26
279	Oct 6	Mark 8:27-38; 9
280	Oct 7	Mark 10; 11
281	Oct 8	Mark 12; 13
282	Oct 9	Mark 14
283	Oct 10	Mark 15; 16
284	Oct 11	Luke 1
285	Oct 12	Luke 2; 3
286	Oct 13	Luke 4; 5
287	Oct 14	Luke 6; 7:1-23
288	Oct 15	Luke 7:24-50; 8
289	Oct 16	Luke 9
290	Oct 17	Luke 10; 11
291	Oct 18	Luke 12; 13
292	Oct 19	Luke 14; 15
293	Oct 20	Luke 16; 17
294	Oct 21	Luke 18; 19
295	Oct 22	Luke 20; 21
296	Oct 23	Luke 22
297	Oct 24	Luke 23; 24:1-28
298	Oct 25	Luke 24:29-53; John 1
299	Oct 26	John 2; 3; 4:1-23
300	Oct 27	John 4:24-54; 5; 6:1-7
301	Oct 28	John 6:8-71; 7:1-21
302	Oct 29	John 7:22-53; 8
303	Oct 30	John 9; 10
304	Oct 31	John 11; 12:1-28
305	Nov 1	John 12:29-50; 13; 14
306	Nov 2	John 15; 16; 17
307	Nov 3	John 18; 19:1-24
308	Nov 4	John 19:25-42; 20; 21
309	Nov 5	Acts 1; 2
310	Nov 6	Acts 3; 4
311	Nov 7	Acts 5; 6
312	Nov 8	Acts 7
313	Nov 9	Acts 8; 9
314	Nov 10	Acts 10
315	Nov 11	Acts 11
316	Nov 12	Acts 12; 13
317	Nov 13	Acts 14; 15; Galatians 1
318	Nov 14	Galatians 2; 3; 4
319	Nov 15	Galatians 5; 6; James 1
320	Nov 16	James 2; 3; 4; 5
321	Nov 17	Acts 16; 17
322	Nov 18	Acts 18:1-11; 1 Thessalonians 1; 2; 3; 4
323	Nov 19	1 Thessalonians 5; 2 Thessalonians 1; 2; 3
324	Nov 20	Acts 18:12-28; 19:1-22; 1 Corinthians 1
325	Nov 21	1 Corinthians 2; 3; 4; 5
326	Nov 22	1 Corinthians 6; 7; 8
327	Nov 23	1 Corinthians 9; 10; 11
328	Nov 24	1 Corinthians 12; 13; 14
329	Nov 25	1 Corinthians 15; 16

DETACH HERE

330	Nov 26	Acts 19:23-41; 20:1;
		2 Corinthians 1; 2
331	Nov 27	2 Corinthians 3; 4; 5
332	Nov 28	2 Corinthians 6; 7; 8; 9
333	Nov 29	2 Corinthians 10; 11; 12
334	Nov 30	2 Corinthians 13; Romans 1; 2
335	Dec 1	Romans 3; 4; 5
336	Dec 2	Romans 6; 7; 8
337	Dec 3	Romans 9; 10; 11
338	Dec 4	Romans 12; 13; 14
339	Dec 5	Romans 15; 16
340	Dec 6	Acts 20:2-38; 21
341	Dec 7	Acts 22; 23
342	Dec 8	Acts 24; 25; 26
343	Dec 9	Acts 27; 28
344	Dec 10	Ephesians 1; 2; 3
345	Dec 11	Ephesians 4; 5; 6
346	Dec 12	Colossians 1; 2; 3
347	Dec 13	Colossians 4; Philippians 1; 2
348	Dec 14	Philippians 3; 4; Philemon
349	Dec 15	1 Timothy 1; 2; 3; 4
350	Dec 16	1 Timothy 5; 6; Titus 1; 2
351	Dec 17	Titus 3; 2 Timothy 1; 2; 3
352	Dec 18	2 Timothy 4; 1 Peter 1; 2
353	Dec 19	1 Peter 3; 4; 5; Jude
354	Dec 20	2 Peter 1; 2; 3; Hebrews 1
355	Dec 21	Hebrews 2; 3; 4; 5
356	Dec 22	Hebrews 6; 7; 8; 9
357	Dec 23	Hebrews 10; 11
358	Dec 24	Hebrews 12; 13; 2 John; 3 John
359	Dec 25	1 John 1; 2; 3; 4
360	Dec 26	1 John 5; Revelation 1; 2
361	Dec 27	Revelation 3; 4; 5; 6
362	Dec 28	Revelation 7; 8; 9; 10; 11
363	Dec 29	Revelation 12; 13; 14; 15
364	Dec 30	Revelation 16; 17; 18; 19
365	Dec 31	Revelation 20; 21; 22

[You have completed the entire Bible-Congratulations!]

DETACH HERE

MAJORING IN MEN® CURRICULUM

MANHOOD GROWTH PLAN

Order the corresponding workbook for each book, and study the first four Majoring In Men® Curriculum books in this order:

MAXIMIZED MANHOOD: Realize your need for God in every area of your life and start mending relationships with Christ and your family.

COURAGE: Make peace with your past, learn the power of forgiveness and the value of character. Let yourself be challenged to speak up for Christ to other men.

COMMUNICATION, SEX AND MONEY: Increase your ability to communicate, place the right values on sex and money in relationships, and greatly improve relationships, whether married or single.

STRONG MEN IN TOUGH TIMES: Reframe trials, battles and discouragement in light of Scripture and gain solid footing for business, career, and relational choices in the future.

Choose five of the following books to study next. When you have completed nine books, if you are not in men's group, you can find a Majoring In Men® group near you and become "commissioned" to minister to other men.

DARING: Overcome fear to live a life of daring ambition for Godly pursuits.

SEXUAL INTEGRITY: Recognize the sacredness of the sexual union, overcome mistakes and blunders and commit to righteousness in your sexuality.

UNIQUE WOMAN: Discover what makes a woman tick, from adolescence through maturity, to be able to minister to a spouse's uniqueness at any age.

NEVER QUIT: Take the ten steps for entering or leaving any situation, job, relationship or crisis in life.

REAL MAN: Discover the deepest meaning of Christlikeness and learn to exercise good character in times of stress, success or failure.

POWER OF POTENTIAL: Start making solid business and career choices based on Biblical principles while building core character that affects your entire life.

ABSOLUTE ANSWERS: Adopt practical habits and pursue Biblical solutions to overcome "prodigal problems" and secret sins that hinder both success and satisfaction with life.

TREASURE: Practice Biblical solutions and principles on the job to find treasures such as the satisfaction of exercising integrity and a job well done.

IRRESISTIBLE HUSBAND: Avoid common mistakes that sabotage a relationship and learn simple solutions and good habits to build a marriage that will consistently increase in intensity for decades.

CHURCH GROWTH PLAN
STRONG - SUSTAINABLE - SYNERGISTIC
THREE PRACTICAL PHASES TO A POWERFUL MEN'S MOVEMENT IN YOUR CHURCH

Phase One:

- Pastor disciples key men/men's director using Maximized Manhood system.

- Launch creates momentum among men

- Church becomes more attractive to hold men who visit

- Families grow stronger

- Men increase bond to pastor

Phase Two:

- Men/men's director teach other men within the church

- Increased tithing and giving by men

- Decreased number of families in crisis

- Increased mentoring of teens and children

- Increase of male volunteers

- Faster assimilation for men visitors - clear path for pastor to connect with new men

- Men pray regularly for pastor

Phase Three:

- Men teach other men outside the church and bring them to Christ
- Increased male population and attraction to a visiting man, seeing a place he belongs
- Stronger, better-attended community outreaches
- Men are loyal to and support pastor

This system enables the pastor to successfully train key leaders,

create momentum, build a church that attracts and holds men

who visit, and disciple strong men.

Churches may conduct men's ministry entirely free of charge!

Learn how by calling 817-437-4888.

SPECIAL NOTE

This book has proven successful with both men's and women's groups, as well as with couples. If you study as a couple outside of a class situation, work separately, then compare notes to see what you've learned. Where you have differences, dig deeper into Scripture, utilizing the *For Further Study* section. Then pray together and come into a place of agreement. Sometimes a troublesome issue early in the book is resolved by the end of the book. If you struggle as a couple, seek your pastor's help.

CONTACT
MAJORING IN MEN® CURRICULUM
817-437-4888
admin@ChristianMensNetwork.com

Christian Men's Network
P.O. Box 3
Grapevine, TX 76099

Great discounts available.

Start your discipleship TODAY!

Call today for group discounts
and coaching opportunities.

FREE DVD!
Send your name and address to:
office@ChristianMensNetwork.com
We'll send you a FREE full-length DVD
with ministry for men.
(Limit one per person.)

ABOUT THE AUTHOR

Edwin Louis Cole mentored hundreds of thousands of people through challenging events and powerful books that have become the most widely-used Christian men's resources in the world. He is known for pithy statements and a confrontational style that demanded social responsibility and family leadership.

After serving as a pastor, evangelist, and Christian television pioneer, and at an age when most men were retiring, he followed his greatest passion—to lead men into Christlikeness, which he called "real manhood."

Ed Cole was a real man through and through. A loving son to earthly parents and the heavenly Father. Devoted husband to the "loveliest lady in the land," Nancy Corbett Cole. Dedicated father to three and, over the years, accepting the role of "father" to thousands. A reader, a thinker, a visionary. A man who made mistakes, learned lessons, then shared the wealth of his wisdom with men around the world. The Christian Men's Network he founded in 1977 is still a vibrant, global ministry. Unquestionably, he was the greatest men's minister of his generation.

Facebook.com/EdwinLouisCole